BETTER BOYS,
BETTER MEN

BETTER BOYS, BETTER MEN

The New Masculinity That Creates Greater Courage and Emotional Resiliency

ANDREW REINER

HarperOne
An Imprint of HarperCollins*Publishers*

Some names have been changed to protect people's privacy.

HarperCollins books may be purchased for educational, business, or sales promotional use. For information, please email the Special Markets Department at SPsales@harpercollins.com.

FIRST EDITION

Designed by Terry McGrath

Library of Congress Cataloging-in-Publication Data

Names: Reiner, Andrew, author.
Title: Better boys, better men : the new masculinity that creates greater courage and emotional resiliency / Andrew Reiner.
Description: First edition. | San Francisco : HarperOne, 2020 | Includes index.
Identifiers: LCCN 2020003439 (print) | LCCN 2020003440 (ebook) | ISBN 9780062854940 (hardcover) | ISBN 9780062854964 (ebook)
Subjects: LCSH: Boys—Psychology. | Masculinity. | Boys—Conduct of life. | Young men. | Child development.
Classification: LCC HQ775 .R44 2020 (print) | LCC HQ775 (ebook) | DDC 155.43/2—dc23
LC record available at https://lccn.loc.gov/2020003439
LC ebook record available at https://lccn.loc.gov/2020003440

20 21 22 23 24 LSC 10 9 8 7 6 5 4 3 2 1

To Elizabeth and Macallah,
my beloved muses and oak beams

CONTENTS

The Age of Reckoning

The hallways hadn't changed at the Sheridan School. There hadn't been any construction or new additions in this K–8 private school in Northwest Washington, DC. And Harrison's head and vision were fine. Yet the then–seventh grader told me, "Sometimes, when I come out of classes, I feel like I don't know where I am. It doesn't last long or anything. But for a few seconds I'm a little, I don't know . . ."

He squinted his eyes and tilted his head, as he often did when he concentrated.

"Disoriented," interjected Nico, his friend and fellow seventh grader.

"Yeah, that's right," said Harrison. "Disoriented."

"Why is that?" I asked.

"Most of the time it feels like this is the school I've always known," Harrison told me. "But sometimes it feels like someplace I've never been before."

Nico nodded.

When you interview people about themselves, often you get a self-conscious, airbrushed version of the truth. Not with these two. They're part of an affinity group—called Boys' Group—that meets once a week to unpack the challenges, complexities, and limitations of traditional forms of masculine identity. (Sheridan offers many affinity groups, including a feminist-focused group called Fem.)

Over the course of a school year, I observed the group three times and regularly interviewed Harrison and Nico.

"Why do you guys feel like you don't recognize this school?" I asked.

Harrison's face flushed, just as it always did when he grew frustrated or upset. "We're constantly being told that we have to watch everything we say and do," he said. "We get it from Fem and from teachers."

"That's true, sometimes," said Nico, who always led with a critical objectivity well beyond his years. "We've had teachers question our understanding of things we discuss in class because we're white males."

Harrison could barely contain himself at this point. "And the girls from Fem make fun of us for being 'girly'!"

On the surface, this middle school baiting may sound harmless (silly, even) enough, but for most males, regardless of age or race, socioeconomic class or classroom, it isn't. I've come to learn it's particularly devastating for early adolescent males. They have to deal with the double burden of establishing a masculine identity, while simultaneously enduring the sting of their peers and often teachers challenging or questioning that burgeoning masculine identity.

Nico shook his head, then looked at Harrison. "That's kinda ironic coming from people who expect sensitivity for everyone else, huh?"

I had never seen Nico as down as I did during this conversation.

After a few quiet moments, he continued, his gaze turned downward. "I've been taught to support women's equality and equality
for people of color since I was in kindergarten. I totally get the need
to 'share the stage,'" he said. "And I agree with all of it. I really do."

"Me, too, mostly," Harrison said, nodding.

"But sometimes it makes me feel like I'm kind of a stranger here,"
Nico said.

"See! It's not just me!" Harrison bellowed, smiling.

From previous conversations with Harrison, I knew that this was
far more than joy at being vindicated. It was relief at—as he often
told me when he examined the benefits of this group—"not feeling
so alone with my own feelings."

Nico continued. "And I've been in school here since I was really
little. I mean, I see girls walking through school wearing T-shirts
that say, 'The Future Is Female,' and I'm like, 'Okay, I completely support feminism.' But where does that leave me? Where does that leave
guys? Where are *we* in that future?"

––––––––

This isn't merely the anxious hand-wringing of an exceptionally
aware and thoughtful middle-school-aged boy. These are the same
existential questions plaguing boys and men of all ages everywhere
today, including those of us who have been struggling for decades to
create healthier expressions of masculinity.

I speak from experience.

I grew up the youngest of four—an older sister, two older brothers, then me. Because my father traveled across the state of Maryland shilling aluminum siding door to door, he was absent from
the dinner table most weeknights. This wasn't always a bad thing,
since our father was a man whose inner demons defined him and

were given full run at the dinner table, where we ate in fear that an incorrectly held fork or a slurp or plates filled with too much food or too little would be met with a full-throttled fury that drove us from the table. My oldest brother tried to fill our father's absence, inciting a reign of terror in his own adolescent male image. He criticized everything we said and everything we did. He sneered at our sister's kind hippie boyfriends. He made fun of our middle brother, who was overweight. I was very young, a highly sensitive and anxious child, and was cowed by anything that suggested failure. If my brother was a wolf, I was his endless supply of limping deer. Nothing goaded him more about me (and informs the way he sees me to this day) as much as a fistfight I got into with a neighborhood boy my age when I was seven or eight. Given how very young we were, it was a brutal, humiliating brawl. Three times this boy commanded me to beg for mercy on my knees and promised to end the fight if I relented; three times I did this, and he responded with yet more blows to my face and head—all in front of the entire neighborhood of kids. When my oldest brother learned about this, he grew apoplectic, deemed me a "disgrace to the family," and never let me live it down. My shame was sealed.

Throughout most of my childhood and even high school, everyone—my friends, my girlfriends, my teachers—considered me easygoing, carefree, and content. But anytime my oldest brother faced off against me on the basketball court or the football field, I summoned an uncommon rage. And on the days I played on his team, I beat myself up afterward for turning the rage I usually reserved for him on the opponents he and I shared. Every time my brother and I teamed up, I secretly embraced, even reveled in, the "Gladiator" team name he openly bestowed upon us. I played with a blinding-red fury and tried to prove that I, too, could dominate my opponent. After those games, I felt queasy and as miserable as the evenings at the dinner table when my oldest brother spat his venom. Why the hell was I trying to impress him of all people? What was I trying to prove?

Though I was loath to admit it as I grew older, deep down I knew why. I wanted to show my brother that I was as tough as he was. That I was just as ready to fight or cut someone down as he was. To my consternation and shame, I recognized that I was trying to show my older brother that I was just as much of a "man" as he was. I wanted him to recognize that I could stand with him shoulder to shoulder—or, if it ever came to it, toe to toe.

The rage my brother inspired in me stayed with me for a long time. Consciously and unconsciously I carried it for years. While I kept my head down throughout high school, during my twenties and thirties I tapped into this rage every time some guy, friend or stranger, tried to impose his hypermasculine agenda on me (sometimes others within earshot). I couldn't let bullying or taunting go unchecked. When I taught middle school, I swooped down with relish on the bigger, stronger, and "cooler" boys anytime they tormented the less athletic, shy, and bookish kids. When I played in thirty-and-over baseball and basketball leagues, my blinding-red fury overwhelmed me when an opponent, or teammate, tried to shame other guys who didn't play at the same caliber as their bellicose teammates. If I was a Gladiator, at least now I was on the "right" team. Right?

It took the birth of my son, Macallah, for me to realize that, regardless of what I told myself, I, too, was guilty of practicing a form of unhealthy, unproductive masculinity that rivaled that of my oldest brother.

I was in the car. I had just finished screaming at—and flipping off—another motorist, when I spotted in the rearview mirror my sweet little boy, tucked away safely in his car seat. A rush of hot shame snaked up my spine, heavy and coiled with regret. Immediately, I knew something had to change—that *I* had to change. I didn't condone this kind of behavior. I didn't like myself when I acted this way, and I hated, absolutely hated, when other men acted this way. So, why was I continuing to act this way?

By the time I pulled the car into our driveway, I had vowed that I would try to tamp down my anger and aggression and, one way or another, start to act as a better model for Macallah. My hope was that if I could learn to be a better man, I could raise a better boy, a sweet and patient and resilient boy, unburdened by the same kind of hang-ups about masculinity I had been lugging around my neck for years.

The problem was, like Nico and Harrison, I didn't know where this left me, or how to move forward. Like them, I also felt disoriented and out of place, unfamiliar with this new territory. Again and again I found that I had a far easier time pushing back against problematic models of masculinity with the same dominate-or-be-dominated mindset than realizing a healthier, more authentic expression of masculinity more in line with the kind of man I wanted to be. But was I really up to the task? For the life of me, I couldn't draw on healthier and more resilient models of masculinity for my own guidance. I couldn't do this because such models were few and far between, too ad hoc or singular for me to hold on to for long.

What started as a personal journey evolved into a deeper exploration of masculinity today—a snapshot of boys and men mucking through new models of masculinity that allow them to thrive. Privately and publicly, in classrooms and in living rooms, on college campuses and behind prison bars, their efforts are starting to reshape and recalibrate masculinity. These boys and men in the vanguard are replacing all-too-familiar masculine expressions with ways of being once considered taboo—such as sensitivity, empathy, and vulnerability—that are, in turn, reaping the very qualities they desperately seek: courage, strength, and emotional resiliency.

What I found was unnerving. Whether or not the Future Is Female, the sad reality is that the Now of Males is decidedly bleak. This is why it's time we start leaning into and learning from these emerging models of masculinity. If we don't, boys and men will continue to stagnate and fall behind.

Or worse.

———

When I began researching this book, I knew that many boys and men were struggling in some parts of their lives. But I was hesitant to call this a crisis or an epidemic. Two years later, I know different.

I witnessed and heard firsthand about this crisis from elementary school teachers, here and in Australia, who told me that they're seeing greater numbers of boys—often as young as six and seven—who are shutting down at their desks when faced with assignments that seem either too difficult or impossible to complete perfectly.

I heard from high school teachers about teenage boys who hand in assignments late or not at all because they'd rather spend their time watching online videos or playing video games or doing something that isn't so "boring," that seems so "pointless" and has little, if any, "relevance" in their lives. I witness this same resistance firsthand at the college level, where my male students are far more likely to fail courses or to drop out of school entirely. Psychologists have a label for this growing number of twenty-something males who either drop out of college or don't attend at all, stay in their parents' homes rent-free, and have little interest in working jobs that "don't pay enough" or that are, they believe, "beneath them": Failure to Launch.

Yes, the untenable rates of anxiety and depression are partly behind boys' stagnation and their inability to stay afloat. But we aren't seeing girls react this way, though they are experiencing the same tsunamis of mental illness, higher rates of anxiety, and comparable rates of depression. At every level of education, they continue to thrive in the classroom, and women are outpacing men when it comes to earning PhDs, medical school degrees, and positions in workplace management.

As if that weren't enough, the pall of suicide looms over men of all ages. Research from the Centers for Disease Control and Prevention (CDC) found that suicidal thoughts and attempts among all children ages five to eighteen have doubled to 1.1 million since 2007. Because this report includes only children who were treated in hospital emergency rooms, this number is far higher, and boys are equal victims in this unnerving public health crisis. At the same time, adult men in their thirties to fifties kill themselves three and a half times more often than do women in the same age range. Most of the conversation about this sobering trend centers around working-class men whose middle-class salaries from careers working with their hands have all but disappeared. But the 2008 recession devastated white-collar professionals, too, especially those in their fifties and sixties, management and finance types in Rust Belt towns, as well as journalists. Earlier this year, my old friend Scott—a highly respected ex–arts journalist for the *Los Angeles Times* and a critically acclaimed book author—committed suicide. Apart from a brief stint with *Salon*, he spent more than a decade actively looking for full-time work. He was fifty and left behind a wife and thirteen-year-old son.

One of the critical factors underpinning the suicide epidemic in men traces back to another epidemic: one-third of American males between the ages of fifteen and sixty-four suffer in physical and emotional isolation. This is leading to one of the biggest public health hazards in Western countries: loneliness. When left untreated for years, loneliness triggers depression, which, increasingly, triggers (loaded verb intended) suicide. In Japan, an entire generation of young men—the *hikikomori*—simply refuse to come out of their rooms.

It's hardly a coincidence that recent spikes in alcohol-related death and disease and opiate and heroin overdose epidemics—public health officials have labeled these "despair deaths"—are affecting men most. And it's not a coincidence that the epidemics of domestic violence and mass shootings are overwhelmingly committed by men.

These statistics are as staggering as they are illuminating.

While boys and men are more than data sets, these statistics speak to the lived experiences of males today. Simply put, there's an ongoing crisis of masculinity, one that extends far beyond the standard *Men Are from Mars/Iron John* framing of years past. A generation-plus of men, I have come to understand, are no longer equipped to thrive in a world that is vastly different from the one our fathers and grandfathers grew up in. We aren't equipped because, consciously or not, we've been practicing and passing along to future generations an outdated model of masculinity that prevents us from realizing our full potential—as fathers and brothers, as husbands and lovers, as coaches and teachers, as classmates and co-workers, and, yes, as the present and future generation of leaders.

The problem is that the old model of masculinity, which champions a do-it-yourself, grin-and-bear-it ethos of emotional stoicism, endless self-sacrifice, and unwavering certitude, no longer serves men—or anyone else, for that matter. The old model no longer works. Not because boys and men today are less worthy of carrying out this model than previous generations. It doesn't work because we continue to expect men to simply *be* these things, at every moment of their lives, without any real guidance or support, which tarnishes any momentary setback or struggle as deficient, unmanly, and unworthy. What's more, the old model prevents them from developing the tool kit they need to thrive and literally survive today—one that requires, among other things, self-awareness, communication skills, empathy, and a willingness to seek help. This, in turn, makes it difficult, if not impossible, for many young boys and men to experience and express the full range of human emotions in an honest and productive way.

As I write this, one of my students is imploding. Like so many of my male students, even in the Honors College at the university where I teach, he hasn't handed in some important assignments, and when he has handed them in they were late. He is struggling at the eleventh hour to nail down the topic and subtopics for a final paper that everyone else is busy completing. During our conversations together throughout the semester (initiated at my request), his despair and the deeper self-contempt he feels have been evident in everything he's done, from his slumped posture to his seized-up facial expressions to the way he averts eye contact. When I asked what was getting in his way, he said, "I just need to knuckle down, work harder."

This is something I hear from a lot of my male students. A strong work ethic is great and something we should *absolutely* encourage in our children. But when a young man is clearly struggling just to keep up with his classmates, and all he can muster is a catchall excuse about knuckling down, he isn't likely to build the kind of resiliency he needs. More likely, he will continue to spiral downward, feeling worse about himself because, on some level, he feels disconnected from classmates and can't move forward. He'll feel like a failure.

The problems facing boys and men today aren't rooted in biology. More and more evidence proves this. The problems they're facing concern gender identity. Even though the right hemisphere of boys' brains develops at a slower rate than in girls—which affects boys' ability to self-regulate their emotions during childhood—this isn't *the* reason they struggle with behavioral issues and coping skills throughout life. The problem is that the way we've conditioned them about how to be a man doesn't exactly help them flourish socially, academically, or emotionally.

On the contrary.

Writing this book, I discovered that the way we've conditioned males to act cuts them off from their parents, their peers, their colleagues, and their partners. More devastatingly, it cuts them off from a deeper understanding and a more complete expression of themselves. (This harmful conditioning was borne out in striking clarity when an acupuncturist told me that her thirty-something husband was glad they had daughters and not sons. "He didn't want to worry about having to be hard enough on a son all of the time," she said.) While interviewing men from all stages of life—from college through middle age—I heard stories about their "fear" and "shame" of needing help and of opening up to male friends about their struggles, which they perceived as failures or personal inadequacies. In this regard, fifty-year-old Bill was no different than twenty-year-old Michael. Both were hamstrung in different parts of their lives by what they both called a "fear of failing." For Bill, this fear manifested in his family life, where he said he "fell short of being the ideal family man" because his wife cheated on him. For Michael, it occurred in school, where he couldn't complete college assignments because he feared low grades.

Despite their thirty-year age difference, neither Bill nor Michael initially turned to male friends or mental health practitioners (or academic tutors, in Michael's case) for help because neither man wanted to "impose" on anyone or expose their own vulnerabilities. Rather than confront and reimagine this limiting gender identity, too many men like Bill and Michael would rather cling to some vestige of "strong" masculinity, even if it means suffering grievously because of it.

As I interviewed males of all ages, I was reminded of the story about Rip van Winkle. While hunting with his dog in the Catskill Mountains, Rip encounters Hendrick Hudson's diminutive, ghostly crew and joins them in ninepins and flagons of a bewitching ale. The next morning, Rip awakens alone, much aged. When he returns to his village, he discovers that twenty years have passed. The American Revolution has occurred, no one in his village remembers him, and everything he thought he knew from only a day before has radically changed. His old tavern buddies are long gone, and his identity as a royal subject no longer serves him. He is irrelevant.

This is what so many boys and men are experiencing today. This is what I experienced when I first started examining my own masculine expressions eight years ago.

Like me, boys and men are still subjugated by a gender identity that they're afraid to challenge, let alone liberate themselves from. Many seem like Rip, dislodged from their past. What happened to the identity that *made sense*? What happened to the easy paths to career, to earning enough to provide a home for themselves and their family? What happened to easy relationships with a partner, children, and friends that didn't require so much work and emotional energy?

John, a forty-something information technology professional, was like many of the men I interviewed. His marriage was falling apart. After an ultimatum from his wife, he sought therapy. What he "suddenly" discovered, he said, was "humbling and a bit shocking." He didn't know how to speak about his feelings beyond anger, and he mostly leaned into the "facts" of his disagreements with his wife. The reason: Over many years of emotion-numbing messages from his parents and the culture at large, he struggled to locate and access his feelings. The pipeline to his deeper emotions had been sealed off. While this didn't impact his job, John eventually discovered that he was depressed, and the relationships that mattered most to him—with his wife and children—lacked emotional intimacy. His relationships suffered because he wasn't able to articulate his own identity, his own humanity, even to himself. Without this invaluable skill set, John had to relearn, with help from his therapist, how to give voice to the feelings beneath his anger and the "facts" and "logic" that masked them.

"Sometimes I really didn't know what I felt," he told me.

It took John some time to face up to it, but he grew to understand and accept something few men ever realize: "The disconnect I had with the most important people in my life started with a disconnect I had with myself," he said. "At home I spent a lot of time in my bedroom, alone. When I did come out, I was surrounded by criticism for just being myself. Until therapy, I never understood why. In my own home, I felt like a stranger."

When we first spoke, John was separated from his wife and sleeping on a housemate's sofa.

Many boys and young men today are having their own Rip van Winkle moment, but the consequences of their reactions are far more noxious to the rest of us. They're doing what men always do when they don't understand the changes going on around them and their identity feels under siege: they're digging in their heels—too often in toxic ways. At the high school level, we're seeing unprecedented sexual violence against younger male teammates. This violence is passed off as sports team hazing practices and is often endorsed by coaches.

At the college level, fraternity participation has been enjoying a 45 percent increase over the past decade, according to the North-American Interfraternity Conference. These Greek organizations are the last-great-safe spaces where young men can teach, practice, and cling to hypermasculine values, especially at largely white fraternities, while enjoying the same social cachet (and, too often, predatory practices) as football and basketball players at big-ticket programs. But these predatory practices aren't exclusive to high-profile athletes or fraternity row. Since 2001, according to one federal study, reports of sexual assault on college campuses have increased by 205 percent, and a recent survey by the Association of American Universities showed that 25.9 percent of female undergraduates—or one in four—had experienced some form of sexual assault.

At the same time, we're seeing a stratospheric spike in the number of right-wing extremist groups, fueled largely by white men who are committing acts of racist, anti-Semitic, and anti-government terror, as these self-perceived marginalized men lash out to protect, as they see it, a dying "patriot's" existence.

Masculinity is at a crossroads. An honest reckoning is long overdue.

———

My research for this book coincided with the rise of the #metoo movement, which accelerated and complicated this much-needed consciousness raising. Seemingly all at once, thousands of women stepped forward to tell their stories about surviving sexual assault and having to endure years of systemic harassment in nearly every professional industry. Their bravery should inspire boys and men alike to take a closer, more honest look at themselves and at our gender's past behaviors that we willfully ignored for too long. The movement also seems to lack patience for open dialogue.

Last year, I spent three weeks as a visiting scholar at three boys' schools in Australia. In addition to giving talks and consulting, I conducted informal focus groups. One group consisted of six high school seniors. Among other things, I wanted to know their observations and feelings about the #metoo movement. All the boys said they supported the movement. One boy, the school's prefect, or handpicked student leader, eventually voiced a general concern of the group. He relayed an experience, I discovered during my research, that was identical to some of his private school male counterparts in America. His school hosted a #metoo dialogue with a girls' school, and he said that girls, understandably, did most of the talking. When he and a few other boys asked some questions about the movement and its ramifications for boys, things didn't go well.

"We were met with furious resentment," he said. "And that's putting it nicely. The girls jumped all over us and criticized us."

Heads around the table nodded.

"If that wasn't bad enough," the boy continued, "administrators here accused us of being disrespectful. Everybody shut us down. But we never meant to be disrespectful. Mostly, we just had questions that the girls wouldn't answer. Did the girls and administrators really think shaming us would suddenly change the way we think?"

On the late nights when such complicated quandaries keep me awake, I never come up with a fail-safe solution. This much I have learned, though: as we continue to show boys and men that girls and women are our equals and should be treated as such, we simultaneously need to encourage boys and men to lean into the most difficult truths about masculinity without harsh judgment from anyone. Otherwise, we'll never start to bridge the divide with women and within ourselves.

Some men have been pushing for this reckoning for a while. Since the late 1960s, many men have been trying to reframe this discussion about masculinity. Their progress occurred in fits and starts and didn't get much traction in the wider culture because, simply, the need wasn't there for most men. Neither was the will to change. Now things are different. We can no longer afford to ignore the crisis that is holding back so many boys, so many men. Too much is at stake. This book attempts to offer a far more dynamic model of masculinity that encourages and empowers boys and men to tap into the full range of their deeper humanity, so they can start to develop the courage, strength, and emotional resilience they need to thrive. To survive.

That's why this book is designed and structured as a masculinity primer. From start to finish, the developmental male arc is explored in depth—in utero through middle age—with a careful eye to the roles of biology and neurology and the profound role that traditional masculine norms play in the lives of boys and men. It's helpful, at this point, to briefly unpack the most common traditional or normative masculine identities discussed in the ensuing chapters. A term that gets tossed around far too often and too loosely, toxic masculinity speaks especially to the *behaviors* men commit that ultimately seek to restore perceived power and control—often with force or violence—when they feel these states are in danger of being minimized or scotched. Beneath toxic masculinity lies hypermasculinity, an identity that's less forgiving of, far less tolerant of, any males who dare to break with its rigid expectations. Boys and men who practice this expression of masculinity secretly, subconsciously obsess—with every waking thought, word, and action—that they might betray the slightest scent of perceived femininity. Acting or dressing or speaking "like a girl" is code for betraying vulnerability, the defining fear of these men. The last normative identity is one I call "static." Males who wallow in static masculinity embrace a bit more fluidity to their masculine identity; men in this camp might hug a friend in public, say, or wear a pink oxford shirt. At the same time, they still practice such hypermasculine traits as refusing to seek help when they need it or to communicate too openly in their intimate relationships, all of which keep them mired in self-destructive habits.

There are essential differences among all three expressions of masculinity; yet too often we group all three under the umbrella of toxicity, which prevents us from having a fuller and more honest conversation about problematic or in-progress expressions of masculinity today. If we're going to get the clearest, most comprehensive take on the central factors that hold back and harm boys and men—and champion the ones that empower us to thrive—it's crucial we examine them separately. Each one carries with it unique challenges and problematic behaviors, and each one offers boys and men different opportunities and approaches for change.

Time and time again, I've heard men complain that embracing the emotional honesty that's core to healthier forms of masculinity would feminize them, make them "too much like women," as an ex-shipbuilder from Bethlehem Steel told me in a Baltimore bar. The best response to such criticism came from Nico, the seventh grader, who has become more resilient since joining Boys' Group and has learned how to understand, process, and discuss his feelings about himself, his relationships, and his place in the world. "I'm still the same," he told me. "But I feel emotionally stronger, more stable. Being in this group has given me more confidence about who I am."

What boy or man doesn't want to feel more self-confidence? Who wouldn't ultimately benefit from this?

But this isn't something we can just recommend for boys and men. Nor can we expect them to initiate this on their own. As many chapters in this book reveal, most boys and men need *permission* from other males they trust and hold in esteem to feel that they can begin this process. Once they do begin it, there's often a considerable learning curve.

"It took me a long time before I could even realize that so many of my deeper feelings were hidden beneath anger and frustration," Ian told me. An architect who's part of a men's group, Ian said that this was true for all of the guys. "We thought that by going on and on about our anger and frustration that we were making progress. But we weren't. We were just hiding behind it."

Once Ian and his men's group grew to trust the male mental health care professional who led this group, they allowed themselves to mine the feelings beneath their anger. "Things started taking off for all of us," he said. For Ian, this meant discovering that many of the romantic relationships that he stayed in for "far too long" weren't ultimately healthy and didn't meet his deeper needs.

As for me, in my attempt to be a better man I am still very much a work in progress.

I continue to struggle to reverse years of learned behavior. I continue to struggle with the difficulty of trying to raise my boy to become one kind of man when the rest of the world—including a lot of women—only seems to recognize and respect the kind of hypermasculinity my brother and literally millions of other men demonstrate every day. And, yes, I continue to struggle with the question of what it means to be a man today, when the world is rapidly changing and starting to demand more from boys and men than ever before.

Still, I try to live up to the promise I made to my son. On the days when cultivating a new expression of masculinity—a healthier breed of Gladiator—feels elusive, too hard, I remind myself of the boys, young men, and adult men featured in this book who are slogging away, too.

The following pages are filled with stories of boys and men like Ian, John, Nico, and Harrison who are doing the hard but essential work of learning to mine and accept the full spectrum of their feelings—the breadth and depth of their humanity—as a way of healing and of becoming more resilient. They are the ones fighting the good and necessary fight. They are the ones paving the way for a bold new masculinity.

One of my aims in writing this book was to paint as full a portrait of masculinity today as I could, so we can start to work together to introduce new models of masculinity that are more in line with our authentic selves and lived experiences. I wanted to meet these boys and men where they were and, through this book, help them—and myself—get to where we so desperately want to go.

During my last interview with Nico and Harrison, they asked me to make a promise.

"What's that?" I asked.

"Make us look good!" joked Harrison.

"Tell the whole story," said Nico. When I asked what he meant, he said, "Talk about how hard it sometimes is to be a guy. So many people today think it's easy to be a guy because of all of the power men have had historically. They still do. But they're also trapped in this Man Box that makes it really hard to grow and be healthier and happier. Make sure people know that we're not all trapped. We're trying to change that."

This is the same promise I made to my son. And this is the promise of the book.

CHAPTER ONE

How We Talk to Boys

The video was only sixty-eight seconds long, but I couldn't stop thinking about it all semester.

A student in the masculinity seminar I teach showed it to me, eager to illustrate for me and the rest of the class the discussion we'd been having about gendered behavior. "It [shows] really well what we talked about last class," she told me, "about the ways adults squelch vulnerability in boys."

The video was shot on someone's smartphone. The frame is vertical and tight, focusing the entire time on an African American toddler. His shirt is off, and he is sitting on an examination table. A health-care professional is readying a series of vaccinations.

As the boy waits, unsure about what is happening, his father tries to get him ready. "You're looking scared," he says. "You're a big boy, right?"

After the boy receives the first shot, pain registers on his face.

The father urges, "Big boy. Big boy." Then his attempt to fortify his son takes on a more serious tone.

"Be a man," the father says.

Over the next few seconds, as the boy's tears increase, something happens.

The father makes an "Arrgh" noise, which sounds less like a pirate's call and more like a linebacker charging a quarterback. "Big boy," the father says, this time with more urgency. "You got it. Don't cry. Be a ma—big boy." As the son gets his next vaccination, the father's hand enters the frame. "High five!" No response. The son lapses deeper into tears, and the father bellows, "Say, 'You a man. I'm a man.'"

And then the tension ratchets even higher. The camera zooms in on the toddler's face. Tears are literally streaming off his cheeks. "Say, 'I'm a man,'" the father demands. Off camera, the health-care worker adds, "Say it loud. Say it loud!" The father continues: "Say, 'I'm a man!'"

Through streaming tears, the boy looks back and forth between the two adults. He slaps his right arm against his side, and, then, amid whimpering and a furrowed brow, from somewhere deep within he conjures a gruff, embattled voice. "Ima man!" he yells, his hand pounding his chest.

There it is.

This video, barely more than a minute long, captures in rapturous clarity how we teach young boys at a shockingly early age to mask feelings of emotional vulnerability and physical pain beneath responses that are more "acceptable" for males.

To be clear, the father wasn't doing anything wrong, per se. He was doing what he thought was best for his little boy.

And yet, what lay beneath his words was the same message many of us tell our boys when they encounter their own fear or emotional discomfort: when the going gets tough, disguise your feelings of vulnerability—fear, pain, shame, or confusion—with defiance, stoicism, laughter, or, perhaps most commonly, anger.

What makes this video clip remarkable, however, is that it captures this dissonance so early in a boy's life. On his contorted, confused face, we see a profound, defining moment in the life of all males— where genuine sadness, pain, and fear are outmuscled by the desire to please a father or respected male with a far more acceptable response.

On this toddler's face, we see something we rarely get to witness: the earliest stirrings of masculine identity at war with itself.

———————

The thing is, infant boys aren't born this way.

Back in the late 1970s and 1980s, Edward Z. Tronick proved this important point. A research associate in the Department of Newborn Medicine at Harvard Medical School at the time, Tronick was interested in levels of emotional and physical stress in infants. To quantify these levels, he and his colleague-collaborators asked mothers to sit directly across from their babies. The mothers were not allowed to express any emotion. Nor were the mothers allowed to talk or coo to their infant children. They had to sit in front of them with a blank, emotionless face for two minutes. This brief interaction triggered high levels of stress in the babies. This approach—known as the Still-Face Paradigm—gauges intimate one-on-one human interaction and is still widely used today.

Tronick employed and refined this technique again many times, particularly during experiments throughout the 1990s while studying stress in infants. In these later experiments, Tronick and his colleagues sequestered mothers from their babies for a brief interval. They then asked the mothers to return and engage with their babies normally, just as they had at the beginning stage of the experiment. This last stage of the experiment was called the reunion.

What Tronick and his team discovered jibed with some of their initial hypotheses: boys had a much harder time dealing with moments of stress than did girls. The boys "displayed more negative affect." They fussed, their facial expressions revealing anger. They twisted and turned in their infant seats, trying to "escape or get away." They gestured to be picked up. In other words, the emotional stress was literally too much for many of the infant boys to bear. There's more. They cried more than the girls and were more likely to look directly at their mothers, express joy, and vocalize throughout the entire experiment, demonstrating, Tronick wrote, that the boys were "more socially oriented than girls."

The infant boys in this experiment behaved exactly as many of us, if not most, would have expected *girls* to behave.

Tronick and his team discovered that infant boys needed more help learning emotional regulation, or "scaffolding" as they called it, than infant girls. What's more, it took longer for boys to "repair" the emotional distance with their mothers during the reunion stage of the experiment. In more recent years, Tronick and his colleagues have examined how infant boys respond to this reunion with mothers suffering from depression, which, as we know, is increasingly common and can manifest apart from postpartum depression, which also is common. The researchers discovered the same struggle in boys. That is, the boys required more time to return to an emotional level of trust with their mothers. At the end of the day, Tronick's decades-long research has consistently popped the bubble on two commonly held gendered stereotypes: boys, it turns out, start out more socially engaged with their mothers and more alert to their facial expressions than girls. Even more crucial to boys' long-term development, they also needed much more calming down and help feeling emotionally secure.

Perhaps the most urgent takeaway from Tronick's research over the decades is this: contrary to the chiseled-in-stone assumptions, boys are not born "tougher," more emotionally resilient, and more self-sufficient than girls. Tronick and his colleagues proved that from the moment they are born, boys are in greater need of emotional support and emotional regulation than previously believed.

This deficit in boys occurs in part due to neurology. In an exhaustive study, Allan N. Schore, author, neuropsychologist, and faculty member of the Department of Psychiatry and Biobehavioral Sciences at UCLA David Geffen School of Medicine, said that the stress-regulating circuits in boys mature more slowly, both in and outside of the womb. So does the right hemisphere of the brain, which is the seat of, among other things, self-regulation and control. "Boys are affected more negatively than girls by early environmental stress," he told me during an interview. "Girls draw on more inner mechanisms for stress resiliency. This is why the attachment with the mother, typically the primary caregiver, is so essential." In his study, "All Our Sons: The Developmental Neurobiology and Neuroendocrinology of Boys at Risk," Schore observed that when mothers aren't attentive enough, infant boys can develop "separation stress," which can cause "an acute strong increase of cortisol and can therefore be regarded as a severe stressor." Ongoing stress in these babies can alter "prefrontal-limbic pathways," which can eventually cause "a variety of mental disorders." Schore's findings have been documented and confirmed by other researchers, including a 2004 study conducted by four Italian researchers in the journal *Personality and Individual Differences*. In the article "Adult Attachment Style and Alexithymia," researchers observed, "There is strong suggestive evidence that the attachment style developed in childhood remains relatively stable across the life span and may even be transmitted between generations."

This is another layer that deepens the discussion about how we talk to, or don't talk to, boys and how it has serious long-term consequences.

This literally changes everything we thought we knew about boys and how we should raise them. Our understanding of boys' emotional lives is entirely wrong. As a result, we aren't raising boys in a way that anticipates or meets their most immediate needs. The problem, as I soon discovered, is that few working models exist today that invite parents and educators to help infant boys, toddlers, and boys develop the emotional scaffolding and resiliency they so desperately require, even into adolescence.

Instead, just like the father in the video, we are raising our boys in a way that neglects their deepest, most immediate needs. Rather than helping infant boys and toddlers develop their own emotional scaffolding, we tell them in moments of great distress and confusion to ignore these very real feelings and pretend everything is fine. We tell them to act *like a man*.

I emailed Tronick about his groundbreaking research, and he put into words what, exactly, had troubled me most about the videotape. "The 'manning-up' of infant boys begins early on in their typical interactions," he wrote, "and long before language plays its role."

From the moment boys come out of the womb, we—their parents, their aunts and uncles, their grandparents, their teachers, their coaches, and, of course, their peers—kick-start a lifelong process of undermining their physical, intellectual, and emotional well-being. Whether directly or indirectly, we are the ones who put certain words *in* their mouths about their identities as burgeoning men. We are the ones who teach them, from an alarmingly young age, to leave other essential words *out of* their mouths.

————

After Macallah was born, one of the first things I did was read to him. I played with him, of course, and I spoke to him a lot. But I was anxious, really anxious, to start reading with him, because I was all too familiar with the crisis of literacy boys face and how it can hold them back later in life. I knew that the earlier you establish "muscle memory" in a boy's neural pathways, the easier it is to make reading a second-nature reflex.

A funny thing happened on my way to my very young son's literacy, however. In almost every book my wife and I read to Macallah, the parent who most often nurtured the young characters was a mother. Almost exclusively, mothers soothed and consoled their young children. Fathers, on the other hand, filled one or more of the familiar roles with sons—doling out admonishments as the starch-collared but fair magistrate; leading the charge on adventures; roughhousing; instigating and indulging goofy behavior and breaking small rules that moms enforced; and, in more contemporary books, playing the part of the cool dude who, although unintentional, hasn't entirely grown up. These fatherly clichés are so pervasive they play out off the page, too, in unexpected places.

The preschool we found for Macallah seemed perfect. Every week he and his classmates were exposed to art, music, and drama. I hoped that this would provide the sort of enlightened male identity that many children's books failed to offer. So when I learned that there was a special breakfast for Father's Day, I was excited. (My wife, Elizabeth, had gone to the Mother's Day breakfast and had come back glowing.)

The children in preschool and kindergarten sat in a circle, just as they did every morning to start their school day. Earlier that morning, during our drive to school, Macallah had told me how he and his classmates had been practicing songs for Father's Day. Finally, I would get to hear my preschool-aged son get the message, from adults other than me, that men weren't limited to the cartoonish stereotypes of fathers. Finally, I told myself, Macallah would hear how fathers were every bit as capable of nurturing their sons with as much sensitivity and compassion as their mothers.

Man, was I naive. I sat in the circle with the other fathers, our children tucked in our laps. The kids serenaded us with a song with the refrain, "Oh, my dad is big and strong." Together, the kids and their dads, beaming to the last one, sang about a dad who "is lots of fun," who lets his child have "second treats." One more thing: "Oh, my dad is really cool." Now, it was powerful to watch and hear the joy in the children as they sang this and to witness the joy in their fathers. And I'd be a bald-faced liar if I said that I wasn't deeply, deeply touched at hearing my son belt out this song with more effort and verve than I heard him sing any other song all year long.

In all of their well-intended innocence, however, these songs managed to capture nearly all of the one-dimensional expectations about how fathers are supposed to act. What I've come to understand, as a father and an educator, is that books and songs—the primary vehicles for communicating values and norms to our young children, in addition to parents and teachers—seep into their consciousness, shaping and defining their perceptions about gendered behavior and, in turn, their expectations about the world and the people in it.

A slow but growing body of research is taking a closer look at the cultural assumptions behind these stories and songs. A 2014 study published in the journal *Pediatrics*, "Gender Differences in Adult–Infant Communication in the First Months of Life," one of the first to closely evaluate both infants' language skills and how caregivers interact with them at birth, revealed some surprising discoveries. Contrary to the prevailing storyline, their research revealed that "infant boys are more vocal [than girls] . . . with a trend for more vocalizations and conversational turns at 7 months [of age]." While the study authors confirmed that mothers speak more and have more vocal interaction with their infants than fathers do, a more surprising and less intuitive finding showed that "mothers spoke more to infant girls than [to] boys in early infancy." Authors Katharine Johnson, Melinda Caskey, Katherine Rand, Richard Tucker, and Betty Vohr found that "Mothers respond preferentially to infant girls versus boys at birth and 44 weeks."

Researchers' response to this discrepancy lies in the projection that girls typically grow into people whose facility with language and emotional intelligence comes more easily, which "may in turn influence greater maternal responsiveness" to them because, hey, it's less work than with boys. If this is true, then mothers are, as demonstrated in Tronick's numerous studies, choosing to interact more with their daughters at a crucial developmental stage—at great cost to boys.

But what about fathers? Two researchers at Emory University's School of Medicine—James K. Rilling and Jennifer S. Mascaro, both of whom work at Emory's Center for Translational Social Neuroscience—examined the language and behaviors of fathers with their toddlers, ages one through three. Rilling and Mascaro focused on fathers because there is far less research about their roles in parenthood than there is on mothers. As one part of the study, fifty-two fathers wore a small electronically activated recorder (EAR software) clipped to their belts twice during the week, both times for a twenty-four-hour period. Once every nine minutes, the device randomly turned on for fifty seconds to record any ambient sound.

Rilling and Mascaro found that fathers sang to and smiled at daughters more often than they did to their sons. Rather than smiling or singing to their sons, they engaged in more rough-and-tumble play. Fathers also were more likely to use words with daughters that were associated with their bodies ("face," "cheek," "belly," etc.). Rilling and Mascaro speculated that this body-focused language introduced in girls a potentially damaging focus on body image. At the same time, the absence of body-focused language around boys can subconsciously separate boys' bodies from their own being, their own sense of self, which could encourage a desensitizing of the human body—theirs and other people's.

One of the findings that deeply unnerved me as a father was what happened when boys called out at night for their fathers. "When a child cried out or asked for Dad," said Mascaro, "fathers of daughters responded to that more than did fathers of sons." When it came to language, fathers used these words more often with daughters: "cry," "tears," and "lonely." They also used more analytical language with their daughters—words like "all," "below," and "much." (Given all of this, I wasn't surprised to learn that a team of British researchers found that Spanish mothers used far more emotional words and emotional topics when speaking with their four-year-old daughters, compared with sons of the same age. Nor was I taken aback to read that fathers used more emotion-laden words with daughters of the same age than they did with their sons.) For boys, fathers used words like "best," "win," "super," and "top." The Emory study attributes these superlatives to "achievement" for boys, but it's clear that that's only part of the dynamic at play. Just look at that list of words: fathers introduced words to their toddler sons that spoke directly to competition and dominance.

When I started researching this book, I reacted with the same dismissive shrug as many people do. Why worry about the way we speak in front of babies and toddlers? Like most people, I assumed that words just go over their heads or that, even if our kids do absorb some of them, they have little, if any, effect. (For all of my conscious effort at using language with my son that leaned into his deeper emotional life, I never gave much thought to words that perpetuate and centralize competition in his identity as a male.) As it turns out, children absorb language immediately, which carries with it some long-lasting repercussions, positive and negative alike.

The *Pediatrics* study from Johnson and her coauthors also found that "early language exposure is important for language development, and children with a rich language environment, specifically infant- or child-directed speech, have better language and cognitive outcomes" for decades beyond. While boys who feel permission to process their deeper emotional experience with honesty enjoy far greater emotional and physical well-being later in life as men, boys who aren't given that permission lack emotional resiliency, which leads to a slew of noxious behaviors down the road. (More on this to come in the chapter about vulnerability.) Over the last twenty-plus years, research mining the disparity in literacy and social-emotional development based on wealth and education has demonstrated that children who hear a steady diet of loving words double the size of their vocabulary compared with children whose linguistic fare is less consistent. These children also enjoy more accelerated social-emotional and cognitive development.

This is why public health officials across the US and Great Britain are developing programs like Talk with Me Baby, a Georgia-based nonprofit organization that teaches parents about the importance of "language nutrition." A big part of the reason for this program is that babies' brains grow approximately 80 percent within their first eighteen months. The impact of adult-child interactions on the brains of infants and toddlers is unparalleled during any other stage of development, because this is when children form the neural connections that construct brain architecture, which is crucial to learning and healthy behavior for decades to come.

The hitch, though, is that much of our emotionally literate and analytical language is still unwittingly funneled to girls—and, as a large body of research has shown, this disparity directly contributes to "consistent findings that girls outperform boys in school achievement outcomes."

The problem in all of this isn't the high proportion of fathers who react and speak to their daughters with emotional literacy. That's wonderful. The problem is that they willfully withhold from their sons the same development-enabling interactions. Fathers who ignore their sons' crying or calling out at night or who purposely avoid using language that reaffirms their sons' deeper emotional identities speak to the same sort of emotional abandonment that the father perpetuated in the video clip of his son getting vaccinated. Yes, he acknowledged his son's pain and fear and tried to talk his son through what was likely his first traumatic experience in the most loving, supportive way he knew. But he met it by utterly dismissing—and, in turn, renouncing—this vulnerability and replacing it with admonitions to, basically, "man up." The fathers in Rilling and Mascaro's study ultimately sent the same message: boys shouldn't require or expect sensitivity or nurturing when they show fear or suffering.

To see if any of the fathers' behavior was hardwired in their brains, Rilling and Mascaro took brain scans of the fathers while they viewed photographs of an unknown child and their own child with alternating happy, sad, or neutral facial expressions. According to Rilling and Mascaro, "fathers of daughters had stronger responses to their daughters' happy expressions in areas of the brain important for processing emotions, reward and value. In contrast, the brains of fathers of sons responded more robustly to their child's neutral facial expressions." In other words, fathers experienced pleasure when they saw their daughters experiencing happiness and had a similar neural response when they saw their sons with a blank, emotionless affect.

Let me repeat that. Fathers experienced as much pleasure seeing their daughters express happiness as they did witnessing their sons express no emotions at all. Not only are most fathers unwilling or unable to meet their son's deeper emotional needs, the average father derives satisfaction when he can ignore them.

When I researched this chapter, I felt vindicated. I was doing right by my son, I told myself; I had springboarded him ahead of many boys his age when it came to a healthier masculine identity that would serve him in all of the important arenas of his life. Since then, the back-patting has stopped. Even if we become more aware of this message we send boys from the moment they're born that emotional language and self-awareness aren't part of who they are in their trajectory as men—and all of the collateral damage this brings—things won't change overnight. Structural change takes time. Until then, boys like my son have to live in a world where they are fighting against a far bigger, stronger current that will try to capsize (or at least dilute) the new masculine identity they're introducing to the world.

———

The Aka are a tribe of hunter-gatherers who live in the tropical rain forests of the Brazzaville region of Congo. Aka men demonstrate a truly singular way of parenting. When mothers aren't around, Aka fathers allow their infants to "nurse" on their own nipples. Unique even among their tribal neighbors, the Aka practice a "fiercely egalitarian" way of life, according to anthropologist Barry S. Hewlett, who has studied the tribe. Male Aka tribe members adopt "roles of the opposite sex." Aka women help tackle and kill game during net hunts, while men contribute greatly to childcare and domestic duties because their survival as hunter-gatherers depends on it. Violence against women is "rare or non-existent," Hewlett has written.

Aka fathers "seek out their infants and infants seek out [them]. Fathers end up holding their infants frequently because the infants crawl to, reach for, or fuss for [them]," writes Hewlett. Fathers don't hesitate to oblige their infants' needs because they "intrinsically enjoy being close" to them. On average, Aka fathers hold their infants an hour during daylight and 25 percent of the time after sundown—both parents sleep with their infants. Conversely, according to studies, American fathers typically begin spending more time around their children once they reach the age of four or five, and when they do "bond" with their sons as babies and toddlers, they typically do so through rough-and-tumble play, as noted earlier. Not so the Aka. Both mothers and fathers opt instead for "frequent caregiving," writes Hewlett, because "vigorous play is not necessary" for establishing deep, affective ties between parents and children.

As a result, Hewlett says, Aka fathers are far more adept at knowing and reading their infants' subtle cues for hunger, fatigue, thirst, and illness. They extend this nurturing-on-demand with older children, too. Hewlett spoke with one Aka father who said that, unlike their farming neighbors the Ngandu, who "love their children only when they are babies," Aka fathers care for their children well into adulthood. "If [my son] is unhappy, I'll look after him, I will cuddle him."

But, as every parent knows, we can't always be there for our sons or daughters. Despite my best efforts to provide Macallah with the emotional scaffolding he needs—and to help him build a level of emotional resiliency to respond to moments when he'll need it—I cannot, unlike the Aka fathers, extend this one-on-one nurturing beyond our home onto the playground or into the classroom, where traditional gendered expectations shove back against it.

Even though my son is still very young, I've been discovering that gender engineering is no match for the pervasive forms of peer pressure about how boys are supposed to act, or who they're supposed to be. When he was in kindergarten, I learned that three boys were taunting Macallah during recess. I found out about it when I saw that he was sullen and distant during our car rides home, which was unusual for him. When I asked him what was wrong, he told me snippets of what was going on—some name-calling, a little pushing during recess, making fun of him for a lot of small things.

That winter I took Macallah to a classmate's birthday party. The children were downstairs, playing in a large den. Three boys were taking turns running into each other, holding a small Nerf football, trying to evade tackle. Most of the time, they just tried to grab the ball.

When Macallah tried to join in, however, they threw themselves at him with abandon. Every time they tackled him, they gave him the ball back and told him to start over again. This went on for twenty minutes, until the boys eventually grew tired of tackling Macallah and left. To my surprise, Macallah called after them. "Hey, where are you going? Let's keep playing!" On the ride home from the party, I talked with Macallah about the need to tell people to stop if they ever did anything to him that made him uncomfortable or scared. "You've told me before that some of the boys in your class sometimes have said or done things that upset you," I said. "Have you asked or told them to stop?" Macallah shook his head. "But why not?" I asked. "Please, please do that next time."

He shrugged.

Later, I asked his teachers if they had observed any taunting; they hadn't. I asked if he fit in with the other boys. (Macallah was the most developmentally immature boy in his class.) They told me that he did little things to try to ingratiate himself—saying or doing inappropriate things that he thought funny—but they often backfired, exacerbating his situation. Despite frequent requests from his teachers to stop such behavior, he wouldn't. More accurately, he couldn't. How can any boy in this culture that deprives him of the emotional scaffolding he needs to self-regulate stop pulling out the only tool he thinks he has when faced with feeling disconnected from his peers? This clearly frustrated one of the teachers, who found this ongoing behavior and his "unwillingness to stop it" disrespectful. This made me wonder if it didn't make it much easier for her to turn a blind eye on the playground. One day, toward the end of the school year, Macallah came to the car on the verge of tears. He finally admitted that the three boys had been hitting his back during recess. "Did you tell either of your teachers what happened like we discussed?" I asked. He shook his head.

For the rest of the evening, I found myself daydreaming about Macallah giving these three boys a good shot to the jaw. Yup, I was reaching for the same gendered expectations I was fighting against when faced with my own son's torment. My head reeled when I considered what my five-year-old son was enduring. Was this really bullying? Bullying didn't happen in kindergarten, did it? Most research finds that it begins later, in third or fourth grade. If all of this weren't hard enough to swallow, something else unnerved me. Despite my frequent entreaties, my little boy wasn't reaching out to teachers and asking for help. What the *hell* was going on? Why would he ignore his father's advice at five years old?

For a week I wrestled with whether to have the conversation that all parents of boys inevitably have to have (or should): if and when he should ever throw a punch. It definitely wasn't a conversation I wanted to have with my very young son. But I knew that it was a reality he would increasingly face with every passing year. The threat of violence in its many forms is the awful yoke every male must bear, even in the renouncement of it, practically every day of his life. Better to start an ongoing conversation about violence now, rather than absolving myself of this responsibility and letting my child learn about it from his peers. I used the "door" Macallah opened on a car ride one day, when he bellowed that he wanted to beat up reckless motorists, to bring up the topic. If another child was hurting him, Macallah should always tell that boy or girl to stop, I said. He should say this once again, if need be. If the aggressor wouldn't stop, and no teacher or familiar adult was within sight, he should try walking away. If that didn't work, I told him, and the other kid pursued Macallah, then he had permission to hit the other child. "Let this kid have it," I said.

Macallah absorbed this instruction with a wide-eyed, caught-in-the-headlights fear as if it had been a blow. For all of his bluster, he didn't want to hit other children, nor did I want him to. It went against everything we had taught him up to that point—the admonition to "use your words." What's more, my child inherited from me a deep sensitivity to which I've always clung, sometimes ferociously. How could I help protect all of this in him at such a young age and, at the same time, instruct him to throw a punch? Not only was I betraying a defining, guiding principle, but I was abandoning him to a terrifying realm to face violence alone. Even if he had been fourteen or fifteen, this philosophical koan would still have befuddled him. The truth is, it made me nauseous and furious to think of my little boy—this beaming spirit who openly hugs and professes his love and gratitude to many people in words and drawings—getting punched in the face because he triggered repressed sensitivity in another kid whose parents taught him to feel shame for it. Self-defense can coexist with sensitivity. But it's going to be a long, hard road getting my young son to understand this complexity—and many ongoing, honest, thoughtful conversations will need to take place.

Apparently, many fathers today grapple with these gendered complexities in their young sons. Judy Chu has studied boys since her graduate school days at Harvard, where she apprenticed under renowned ethicist, psychologist, and feminist scholar Carol Gilligan. After an eye-opening conversation with a friend of her younger brother, Chu, an affiliated faculty member at Stanford University, told Gilligan about the underrepresented research on boys and men. Gilligan suggested that she look at when boys first start absorbing the norms of traditional masculine identity. For girls, this identity adoption begins early in adolescence at approximately age eleven or twelve. For boys, the gender expectations begin disturbingly earlier.

"Many fathers today face a paradox when their sons enter school," Chu, the author of *When Boys Become Boys*, told me. "They may cherish the sweetness, the sensitivity, the thoughtfulness in their little boys, and they know these traits will serve them as adults. But they also understand that these traits put them at risk of being teased. They don't want their boys to be targets on the playground."

So, fathers who openly practice a newer brand of masculinity, or even just secretly covet sensitivity in their boys, watch their sons lose the very thing they want most for them.

What further exacerbates this new course of identity for boys is the concrete stage of development they experience at this age. This two-dimensional way of seeing the world makes the "rules" they're suddenly learning from peers and older children that much more binary and rigid. (As if that weren't enough, this is also when many children first learn to conform to satisfy the nascent yearning to fit in.) Most important, they're faced and strapped with this ethos at such a young age, there's no way they could ever realize that there are different ways to express their masculinity. "This happens so early," says Chu, that "on some level they believe this is the way the world is."

What boys do eventually realize, though, is that they have to learn how to navigate this minefield if they want to fit in to most school environments—what to say, when to say it, and who to say it to, especially in front of other boys. It's a communication model that squares perfectly with the void of deeper emotional awareness and honesty they learned from parents and other caregiving adults very early in life. They learn to "protect themselves out of necessity," says Chu. "[When] boys start school, suddenly they have to develop an awareness of the expectations—an awareness of the consequences of deviating from those expectations. And there are consequences." A boy in kindergarten or first grade has to remember who he can cry in front of, who he can tell that he's scared or confused. If not, he might face teasing and rejection for contradicting the concrete, one-dimensional masculinity that most boys have been taught—and that too many of them will protect and practice to devastating effect well into adulthood.

Some fair questions come to mind at this point. Isn't it good that boys learn this crucial life skill earlier rather than later because they'll just have to learn it later, anyway, right? Well, yes, but five- and six-year-old children aren't equipped to negotiate the pressures, let alone the complexity, of such Byzantine social and emotional identity issues. And this: aren't boys just facing the same intense peer pressure that girls face? Yes and no. Girls absolutely have to negotiate intense, crushing peer pressure, but they encounter it later, during third or fourth grade, when they are developmentally more mature (girls are already more mature than boys on many levels). The peer pressure they face is more relational. Little boys face overwhelming pressure to renounce their *sense of selves as males*—to accept an identity that wholly rejects the very sensibilities that many adults still want for them. This is why when I hear adults call Macallah or other young boys "Little Man," I want to respond, "Please don't call boys this. You have no idea how damaging it is."

Perhaps nothing else sums up boys' plight as well as something a boy's mother told Chu during her research: "What adults think of as play and fun for boys is actually a lot of work."

CHAPTER TWO

Boys to Men

My initial interview with Taylor, a senior at Towson University, played out the way interviews usually do with guys his age, with vague, evasive descriptions of things that bothered him. When I asked about his high school experience, Taylor mentioned a girlfriend but spent more time talking about his relationships with other males. On some days, he told me, he was "bummed" because a few guys at school would "ride" him about "something." When he uttered these things, I didn't give them a second thought. After all, such elusive terms are just the way many guys speak about their lives.

A closer reading of my notes later that night, however, revealed something: like many adults, I had glossed over the generalities of Taylor's responses, assuming little lay beneath them. I trusted that he was responding to my questions with transparency and, perhaps more important, that he had access to the words to convey how his experiences affected him.

I had to remind myself that most males speak in a coded language that obfuscates the truth, particularly when the conversation concerns their personal and emotional lives. This became clear when I read two things Taylor had shared earlier that day. "I had to figure out a lot of things about being a man by myself," he had told me. When I asked him if there was a superhero he admired, he answered without hesitation, "Captain America. He doesn't back down from his morality and his commitment to protecting other people, especially people who are vulnerable."

Taylor was one of many college- and high-school-aged boys I interviewed in an effort to better understand how boys and young men were engaging with older, more static forms of masculine identity and to what extent, if any, they were integrating newer permutations of it. After all, millennials and Gen Zers have far more nuanced forms of gender identity, and in line with that, they place a high premium on individualism. For many of them, all of this translates into a need to customize their gender identities. Since there is a dearth of research about how boys and young men express their masculinity, or even feel about gendered expectations, I wanted to hear, firsthand, what it's like navigating and mashing up against traditional models of masculinity. One of the things I've observed while teaching at the college level is that, unlike their female peers, many boys and young men don't articulate and work at regulating their considerable emotional stress and duress—their vulnerability— in healthy ways. As a result, they don't seem to be thriving either in or outside school. To get a fuller picture, I solicited volunteers on campus. Taylor was the most willing of these respondents.

Thankfully, he agreed to a second interview. He also agreed to clarify some of his initial responses, which was helpful because I was also curious to explore the connection between Taylor having learned how to become a man on his own and his passionate admiration for

Captain America, a paragon of masculine virtue and righteousness. Taylor, an Asian American in his early twenties, told me that he was adopted by white parents and that he never identified with his father's more traditional model of masculinity. "He pushed me as a kid to be a hypermasculine man's man—to be aggressive, competitive, and to play sports." His father never comforted Taylor when he cried, nor did he answer questions about dating when Taylor expressed his curiosity. The only emotion Taylor saw his father express openly was anger. "When I was four my dad hit me. He slapped me around. Even then, I knew it wasn't always for punishment. He'd take his anger out on me. When I told my mom about it when I was a little older, she said it was because his boss was trying to get him fired." Taylor said his father hit him on at least six or seven different occasions.

Whenever Taylor touched on something that had deeper painful resonance for him, he laughed, tilted his head a bit, and pounded a clenched fist into his other palm, emphasizing his point. It was done unconsciously, lightly, the way people fist bump. Still, a clenched fist is a clenched fist. He did this often when we discussed his high school friendships. The "something" that "bummed" Taylor, I learned during subsequent interviews, turned out to be a form of bullying that followed him for all four years of high school. And it came from an unlikely place—his cross-country teammates.

"They alienated me for being Asian, for being shorter. I was quiet and had no, I mean no, social skills," he said, erupting into laughter.

He told me that, even though his school was largely white, the other Asian American kids were "outgoing, confident. They all were accepted into other friend groups."

I asked Taylor if he thought his teammates were deliberately targeting him. "I don't think they were trying to be mean—not purposely, at least," he told me, still laughing and pounding his open palm.

In the face of the taunting, Taylor stood his ground. "I wouldn't react to any of it. I just thought they were pushing my limits." During breaks in practice, though, he began feeling the weight of this bullying. "I told myself that I shouldn't feel this way. They're just jokes, right?" he said, switching into present tense. "But why are they hurting so much? They're just jokes."

Every day when he got home, he would go into his room, close the door, and cry. This triggered a cascade of dark thoughts, which played off of each other. First, Taylor got down on himself for crying, which only caused him even more guilt and shame for being so "weak," as he said. That, in turn, drew even more waves of self-loathing—more feelings of weakness, shame, and guilt—as he stepped outside himself and judged the way he *responded to his response.*

In his growing isolation, Taylor came only to this conclusion: "I was a bad person for reacting this way. So, I put on a mask, pretended everything was fine, but pushed everyone away when it came to this problem."

Looking down and shaking his head, Taylor told me with a curt laugh, "I contemplated suicide."

Taylor's story reflects a revealing portrait of many boys' and young men's lives today.

Beneath his incisive insights about the dangers of his father's kind of hypermasculinity, lay dusty gender expectations about how men are supposed to act during moments of emotional distress and uncertainty. It's an unconscious colliding between parts of static masculinity that don't jibe with their newer, more dynamic, healthier masculine identity. The problem is, like Taylor, most boys and young men don't even realize that they are captive to the same stagnant values they so eloquently rail against.

While it's true that boys and young men today are more concerned than previous generations with issues of racial and gender equality and are far more willing to express their individuality than their fathers are, they haven't figured out how to break free completely from outdated models of masculinity that are proving far more detrimental to them than to the men who continue to swear by them. True, he never bought into the hypermasculine trappings that his father modeled. Like too many boys and young men, though, he still couldn't muster the courage to escape some of the most lethal ones: he didn't think he was supposed to ask for help, and even if he wanted to, he literally didn't know how to ask for it. Unable to articulate a healthier model of masculinity, which would have allowed him to give voice to his isolation and alienation, Taylor was stuck between his father's emotionally closed-off model and one that would allow him to express the full range of his emotions and, in the process, the full range of his humanity.

Like so many young men (even men well into their thirties), he embraced models of masculinity from popular culture: fictitious men who, while displaying a few vulnerabilities for greater believability, exude cocksure, muscular confidence and are men of action who don't ask for help when they suffer. These are the legacies of static masculinity that create shame in many boys and young men who believe they are complete failures as ascending men for not flexing these qualities when faced with life's problems. This legacy nearly killed Taylor.

He's far from alone.

An exploding number of millennials and Gen Zers are becoming incapacitated by depression and anxiety. The CDC conducted a study that found that, since 2007, suicidal thoughts and attempts among children ages five to eighteen have more than doubled, and self-reported suicide attempts have skyrocketed by 73 percent among African American boys and girls in high school. Some critics insist that the reason for this lies in awareness; we are more cognizant of mental illness symptoms than we used to be.

If you have taught in a high school or college over the past fifteen or twenty years, you know that this uptick is empirical—it's difficult not to see the sea change if you're paying attention. A survey of 63,000 students at ninety-two schools conducted by the American College Health Association found that nearly 40 percent of respondents felt so depressed that it was "difficult to function," and 61 percent said they felt at least one instance of "overwhelming anxiety" in the prior year. Many studies and articles over the past six or eight years have attributed this mental illness, in large part, to the relationship these generations have with social media and the attending terror that comes with FOMO (fear of missing out). Lord knows there's truth behind this. But there's more to this mental illness than meets the eye. New research is bearing out an obsession with perfection—with one's own achievements, with social perfection, and with an insistence on perfection in others' behavior.

These three tiers were fingered as the culprits in a study conducted with 41,641 American, Canadian, and British college students who completed the Multidimensional Perfectionism Scale, a test that gauged generational changes in perfectionism from the late 1980s to 2016. The study, published in the journal *Psychological Bulletin* and conducted by Andrew Hill and Thomas Curran, found that college students today have been inculcated with the belief that perfection is essential in all parts of their lives. When it came to a need to appear perfect in their social lives, for instance, contemporary college students' scores rose 33 percent. "These findings suggest that recent generations of college students have higher expectations of themselves and others than previous generations," said Curran. "Today's young people are competing with each other in order to meet societal pressures to succeed and they feel that perfectionism is necessary in order to feel safe, socially connected and of worth."

In an article about this trend, Reef Karim, who runs an outpatient clinic for addiction in Beverly Hills, observes that, despite their vast social networks, "Millennials tend to be more isolationist" and have "less social armor."

For young men—who are the least likely to seek mental health assistance, or any kind of assistance, lest they appear incompetent as men—this isolation makes them even more vulnerable. Not less.

In their groundbreaking book, *Raising Cain: Protecting the Emotional Life of Boys*, authors Dan Kindlon and Michael Thompson observe that "many boys struggle alone with their distress because they think they have to, or they think they can 'fix it' themselves." There isn't a parent or teacher who would suggest that clinical depression is character-building for boys, and yet boys are expected to 'get over it' on their own.

What ultimately saved Taylor was a small group of guys on his cross-country team. These four guys—"in-betweeners who didn't fit into any other social group"—became his friends and eventually began standing up for Taylor when their teammates started bullying him. "Without them, I don't know if I could have made it through," he said. His inclusion into their social group was slow, starting first with smartphone group chats. Over time, those seemingly minor interactions led to face-to-face get-togethers, and eventually the cloud lifted. "My life didn't have any value, but these guys valued what I had to say. They recognized that I was closed off, but they included me to hang out on weekends." Taylor still struggled with his psychic and emotional pain because he was afraid his new friends would consider him "weak" if he opened up about his depression and suicidal ideation. For a while, the group kept "it light" and didn't discuss deeper feelings, but Taylor eventually discovered that "feelings of sadness [and] depression were common for all of us, which was a really big help to me."

During his senior year in high school, a friend in his calculus class introduced him to a pickup artist website, which he told me helped him learn more about himself. When I shared my hesitations about pickup websites, which are often rooted in misogyny, Taylor insisted that the "toxic, creepy" side of this subculture wasn't the appeal for him. Oddly enough, some of what he gleaned from the website helped him develop a "purpose and motivation I wanted but didn't have before." It also taught him about the importance of "being happy with yourself" and having "a life going for yourself before you introduce girls into the mix." Having taught him for two semesters in the Honors College, and having gotten a sense of who he was from his writing assignments and from his interactions with female classmates, I could believe this.

That's when I realized Taylor had nowhere else to turn when he had important questions and needed guidance in his burgeoning sexuality. So he did what most boys do—boys who don't even turn to their fathers with questions about life's dilemmas: he sought out advice from a peer with little life experience. The friend who introduced Taylor to the world of pickup artists started organizing regular get-togethers with a new group of friends. During school breaks, the participants met up and sat in a circle in someone's den or basement, held a TV remote control, and performed mental health check-ins. The one holding the remote control posed a question to the group, which everyone had to answer honestly. A recent question, typical of the group's topic of conversation, went something like this: "On a scale of one to ten, rate your mental health right now and explain why it's where it is."

Taylor told me this meeting was a "huge help" both in the classroom and out of it. His grades began to more consistently reflect his ability and effort, and this seemingly goofy circle check-in propelled him to seek out the self-help teachings of Jack Canfield and Tony

Robbins when his depression became overpowering. "I adore these guys," he said, growing visibly animated. "They've become mentors for me, giving me guidelines for how to live and further drill down my purpose in life." This even led him to attend a Tony Robbins seminar, where, amid sleep and nourishment deprivation, dancing and shouting positive affirmations, he learned the value of a "positive mind-set" and "gratitude." Now he keeps a gratitude journal, which he updates every night, ending the day on a positive note. "The clouds of depression are always there," he said, "but when I do all of these things, they start to dissipate. And I can see who I'm supposed to be."

What ultimately saved Taylor—and continues to save him as he struggles with depression—is something few boys and young men are lucky enough to have.

———

For a while now, I've wondered how high schools are preparing boys for life, because school is *the* defining space where boys and girls spend so much of their lives. This is where so much of their existence is shaped, for better and for worse, by both unscripted events and interactions and by the grand designs of teachers and administrators. And, let's face it, whether they want to or not, more and more teachers are becoming surrogate parents and social workers for their students. The few schools around the country that seem to be paying attention to what boys need largely consist of single-sex charter schools geared toward boys of color and private boys' schools. These schools emphasize, among other traits, accountability, humility, respect, self-reliance, and courage. What they're trying to do, as many of their brochures and websites insist, is "prepare men" to take "leadership roles" in the twenty-first century. Put another way, many of these schools are trying to pick up where so many fathers left off a long time ago when young men first left family farms during the industrial revolution—by instilling in their charges traditional male rites of passage. There's no question that many boys today can benefit from learning such traits, especially if they help boys who are maturing much later to develop the focus and motivation needed to keep pace with girls in the classroom. (We're not only talking about competition with girls; the point is also to help boys keep up with them.)

Since the mid-1990s, we've been having a conversation about the growing decline of boys' performance in the classroom. Depending on your worldview, the reasons vary—from the purported differences in hard-wiring between the sexes to the increasing feminization of classrooms, which play to girls' strengths, to the lack of male teachers at lower grades to assigned books whose introspective sensibilities don't appeal to most boys. It's absolutely true that most boys need more wiggle time and that their language skills develop later than do girls', a cognitive difference that isn't helped by unrealistic Common Core standards that ignore these very real neurological differences between boys and girls. In reality, boys have been losing ground to girls in the classroom incrementally since the mid-1970s, a disturbing trend that continues into college.

Research shows that most people learn more effectively and pull down better grades when they're actively engaged during class. This is especially true for students who don't understand the material or who distance themselves emotionally because they dislike the teachers or subjects or feel shamed. Ultimately, this compromises their ability to form and articulate questions and insights on the spot, a skill that's essential in the workplace and, at times, in personal relationships. This is especially true for boys.

Beau Dagenais is keenly aware of how masculine identity can get in the way of learning for guys. Dagenais, an English teacher at Boys'

Latin School of Maryland, a single-sex independent school, says that he aims to get students to "break out of the restraints these guys have set for themselves." He has zeroed in on what he perceives to be one of the factors holding boys back from learning: their lack of questions.

On the surface, reluctance to ask questions might not sound like a big deal. After all, how could something as small as a question make a dent for boys and young men when it comes to something as large as helping them become better risk-takers in the classroom?

The answer requires a little bit of unpacking. For starters, the American educational system, and its growing dependence on teaching to the formulas of standardized testing, undermines intellectual curiosity. In such a binary system, only "right" and "wrong" can coexist, a terrifying proposition for teens weaned on a culture of perfection in their texting, social media, sports, body image, and academic lives. This is a generation that feels safer crafting and editing text messages than talking on the phone or in person because they fear the messy imperfection of conversation. Add to this mix a gender script that demands that males appear decisive, make decisions quickly, and plant a flag in certainty. It's no wonder that so many boys and young men either cop a yawning, disaffected disposition in the classroom or can't stop raising their hands and imposing their worldview. Both reflexes speak to the fear festering beneath the veneer.

Is it any wonder that by high school boys stop asking questions in school? The whole premise of openly courting curiosity and intellectual uncertainty flies in the face of gender identity for many young men. This was summed up with perfect precision for me by an educational researcher: "Girls seek to improve, while boys seek to prove."

An increasing body of research is bearing this out. In their book and a report under the same name, *The Rise of Women: The Growing Gender Gap in Education and What It Means for American Schools*, sociologists Thomas DiPrete and Claudia Buchmann insist that boys' underperformance in school has more to do with society's norms about masculinity than with anatomy, hormones, or brain structure. In fact, boys involved in extracurricular cultural activities like music, art, drama, and foreign languages report higher levels of school engagement and academic performance than boys not involved with those extracurricular activities. But these cultural activities are often denigrated as unmasculine by preadolescent and adolescent boys—especially those from working- or lower-class backgrounds, according to men's studies guru Michael Kimmel. In his book *Manhood in America*, Kimmel argues that it's the "ideology of traditional masculinity that keeps boys from wanting to succeed. Boys see academic success itself as a disconfirmation of their masculinity."

A 2015 paper, "High School Boys, Gender, and Academic Achievement: Does Masculinity Negatively Impact Boys' Grade Point Averages?," quantified this. Researchers from Ohio State University found that gender identity plays a large role in boys' performance. They observed that across the board, both racially and socioeconomically, "masculinity is associated with a significant decline in overall GPA."

Nick Rego, who teaches English at McDonogh School in Baltimore, a coed independent day school, noted that the girls in his AP classes are much more engaged than the boys. He said he wishes boys would ask questions more regularly—but with one catch. He wants them to do so during class. "Nothing is lost by them coming to me after class. But in class discussions about complex ideas something is lost. If they're passively engaged, they lose the skill to articulate a question in the moment. They lose the ability to say what they're thinking. It's a self-reinforcing cycle where girls get better at asking questions and saying what they're thinking."

So, the prospect of getting male students to embrace questions as an integral part of learning as they get older is nothing short of revolutionary. For Dagenais—whose students venerate him and seek out his counsel like Robin Williams's character John Keating in the film *Dead Poets Society*—it is business as usual. "This is the way I approach life and the world," said Dagenais, who made this connection a few years into his teaching career. "I started to see how masculinity could be a thing that could be affected by this."

Dagenais doesn't want to perpetuate the tongue-tied rigidity in his students. He directs his male students toward questions they have about a topic at hand during discussions. "I'll celebrate the great question that comes up during class." He even gives as much weight in grades to an unfinished essay as he does to a polished essay—if it shows genuine curiosity and risk-taking with "ambiguity" in exploring an idea or concept. He's more likely to write on an essay "Great job with these questions!" than he is to compliment a narrow, well-fortified argument.

This applies to tests, too. Instead of looking for answers, Dagenais includes a prompt that asks, "What would be a great question to ask that comes out of this reading?" He says, "I'm trying to model the same curiosity I ask of them."

By Dagenais's own admission, he's pushing back against the educational status quo with an approach that elevates process over product. He thinks students respond to it. "Teenage boys smell bullshit better than anyone." He says that many of his students don't trust or find value in a system that places letter grades over practical application. "They are craving meaning, capital 'M.' Grades don't give them meaning at this point—they leave them feeling empty."

By leaning into process, Dagenais is also helping his students head in this direction. Learning how to question opens a portal to more intimately probing their lives and their place in the world—and what it really means to "be a man."

"Something I spend a lot of time on is getting the guys to admit uncertainty, to embrace ambiguity," says Dagenais. He wants them to learn how to admit to others—and to themselves—"Maybe I'm wrong." This process pays off. "By the end of the year," he says, "many of them have a different lens through which to see the world. They become more compassionate and empathetic. Some kids who have an aggressive masculine edge at the beginning of the year become softened in really good ways. They learn to listen to others and themselves in a different way." Just as important: "They learn to change their minds."

The existence of schools that pay attention to what boys need is encouraging. The problem, though, is that precious few of these schools look beyond this threadbare code of manhood to embrace the other traits that boys and men *also* need in the twenty-first century, traits that best teach and develop personal responsibility, empathy, self-awareness, maturity, and emotional authenticity. These traits are integral and need to be part of the new rites of passage because they develop resiliency from the inside out. The few schools that lean into teaching boys emotional authenticity are seeing powerful, immediate results.

Three years ago, I visited a private boys' school in Baltimore to meet with members of the upper school faculty and administrators. They were kind and gracious enough to discuss whether they had noticed a decrease in the emotional resiliency of their male students, something I had noticed in my college classroom for a while. Regardless of gender, none of my students were doing well. Though clearly intelligent and hard-working enough, they struggled day to day. A handful of the young women missed classes every semester because

of anxiety and panic attacks, but they still pushed through and completed their work. This wasn't the case with my male students. Many
of them weren't handing work in on time or weren't getting it done
at all. Many spent all of their energy and intellect finding ways to cut
corners—alibis, flat-out lies, and, the big one, procrastination—to
get out of doing the required work.

The faculty and I gathered in a dark-wood-paneled room with
hunter green carpeting, reminiscent of the sanctuaries evoked in
films about prep schools where "discretion" trumps transparency,
and introduced ourselves over lunch. A few of the faculty members
and an administrator said that they had, in fact, noticed a "blip"
in the resiliency of their all-male student body. As we sat in a large
square, the upper school counselor said she was witnessing this
problem among some graduates. Two or three who had graduated
the previous year dropped out of college and came back home.
She had spoken with these boys and their parents. "They weren't
equipped to problem-solve," she offered without hesitation, as her
colleagues focused on finishing their lunches. "They didn't seem to
be aware of where to find the resources they needed." This counselor echoed a dichotomy that exists among many parents (and educators): some of them make boys too independent and unwilling
to seek help when they need it, while others exert too heavy a hand
and don't allow them to take risks and fail.

I asked her if she had ever worked with girls before. She said that
she had worked for seven years at a preeminent all-girls institution
in Baltimore. When I asked her if she noticed any difference in the
way girls handled new challenges or problems, she said, "I saw much
more proactivity from the girls." Most of her colleagues had finished
their lunches by now, and a few looked uneasy when she made this
comparison. "They're much quicker to self-advocate," she added.

"Is it possible," I asked the entire group, "that maybe the way your male students are taught to handle challenges might contribute to their struggles in and outside of the classroom?" The raised eyebrows and throat-clearing around the square made it clear: I was an outsider, and I had definitely crossed a line. Like fallen dominoes, each one of them collapsed behind the same response—one by one they discussed all of the things they were doing right to make their students resilient.

A young upper school administrator, also a teacher, said that he taught his students the same life lesson his teachers had taught him at his private high school. At some point every year, he told me, he wrote it down on the dry-erase board, then he read it aloud: "K-W-T-D-W-Y-D-K-W-T-D. Know what to do when you don't know what to do," he said with obvious pride. From the corner of my eye I noticed one of his colleagues looking downward and shaking his head. "How does this make them more resilient?" I asked. "Because it teaches them the value of preparing ahead of time," the administrator explained. "We teach resilience through preparation."

"But how can you possibly teach them to prepare for things they can't anticipate?" I asked.

He flashed a bemused smile. "Of course, there's no way to prepare boys for every curve ball they face. But I give them a framework to start from, so they know how to approach and react to life's problems."

"Do you teach them mindfulness techniques?" I asked. "Because, you know, research shows how it prevents reactivity and encourages clearheaded thinking and problem-solving."

Blank stares greeted my question.

Looking around the room, I continued. "And we all know how impatient and reactive many boys can be, right?"

"Yes, I know about its value," the administrator replied, "but that's not what I emphasize. I encourage them to look for answers. To think about possible solutions."

Heads around the room nodded.

Again, I noticed his colleague. This time his eyes were turned up-ward, and he was shaking his head slightly.

Who would question this dedicated educator's motives? He clearly wanted what was best for his male students—to encourage a calm, logical, solutions-based approach when life's challenges arose. But something about this approach also felt a little too dogmatic and inflexible.

A week later I reached out by telephone to the teacher who had shaken his head. I asked him why he had done this when his colleague had shared his mnemonic. "Because it completely ignores—worse discounts—the need for time and space when dealing with life's com-plexities. And, let's face it, these guys live in a very complex world. The last thing we should be encouraging in them is the need to look more 'manly' by feeling pressured to have answers at the ready when problems arise. I find that the first, best solution to complex problems is asking questions. This kind of thoughtfulness is more crucial to preparing them for life than forcing an answer for the sake of having one."

The tension between these two educators spoke to a larger phil-osophical difference in what we think boys and young men need in preparation for life. The upper school administrator was, ulti-mately, championing the same stoic-doer masculine identity that Taylor's father and many others model: the man of action, the man of answers—the man who figures out what to do when he doesn't really know what to do.

When I conducted four small focus groups among juniors and seniors in a psychology class at another private boys' school in Balti-more, I asked questions about masculine identity. One of the themes I heard a lot centered around control. Men should always have an an-swer to a problem, I heard over and over. When I asked the students what they most valued in their male friendships, nearly 60 percent of the forty-eight boys who participated liked that their male friends offered solutions when they presented them with personal problems. "We want practical advice, solutions," a junior told me to the nods of his classmates. "Not emotional support."

I came away from those groups understanding for the first time why my male college students so often embrace muteness, as these boys did. They fear appearing male-imperfect. That is, they will remain silent unless they are certain they can pony up some bons mots or "correct" insight about the topic at hand. Anything less makes them appear inadequate, which leaves them feeling vulnerable, something they want to avoid at all costs.

Many of those who want boys and young men to always have "the answer" don't understand that the prefrontal cortex in male brains doesn't start to reach maturity until at least their mid-twenties, or even later today. Encouraging boys and young men to have all the answers at an early age sends them the message that sifting through the complexity of a problem and its options will give them less credibility as a "man" than scrambling for an answer and boasting about it with porcelain confidence. Perhaps no other narrative in the script weighs as heavily on boys and young men in the classroom.

But there are other, more urgent and far-reaching, reasons we shouldn't lean on boys to obsessively dwell on "right" answers. So much about the static masculine ethos we encourage in boys, and eventually men, teaches them that they need to always have a response at the ready, one that's "right" or at least funny or sarcastic enough to command laughter. Yet this mindset undermines their willingness to take healthy risks in learning—the very kind of risk-taking that girls are encouraged to do and that they, to their considerable credit, excel at. Far too often, the message boys learn in school is one of self-denial. Boys are taught to renounce the deeper parts of their being that might betray the thin, scowling veneer of resiliency we consider "manly." If we want to make boys more resilient in a way that will benefit them in school and beyond, we need to teach them how to remain more flexible, curious, and open to risking the right kind of failure.

No research has been done yet to gauge boys' feelings about gender expectations at the elementary school level, but a recent public opinion study of 1,006 adolescents ages ten to nineteen, funded by Plan International USA, revealed some sobering findings. While girls are finally (*finally*) feeling far more empowered and less constricted by old limiting gender expectations, boys and young men are still straitjacketed. Male participants said they receive messages from adults that society most valued these traits in men: "honesty, morality, ambition, and leadership." Beyond lip service, though, these weren't the expectations adults or their peers pinned on them.

In the research, boys ages ten to thirteen said they feel pressure to be physically strong and to play sports. The stakes get higher for boys ages fourteen to nineteen, who feel most pressure to appear physically strong, to play sports, to be willing to "punch someone if provoked," and to "dominate" other males. A third of adolescent boys believed they should "hide or suppress their feelings when they feel sad or scared."

Perhaps most revealing, nearly half of the older boys said they "want to learn more" about having the "right" to feel all of their emotions.

This sounds like science fiction—some Star Trek race of beings who have been deprived of a basic instinct or function common to humans: the permission to learn how to experience all of their emotions. There's something deeply sad and centrally debilitating about this. Little wonder that boys and, especially, young men experience masculine identity like it's some chronic illness. "It's never-ending," said Ryan, a junior at Towson University in Baltimore. "Whether I'm sitting in class, at a party, or working out, I'm constantly worried. Am I coming off the right way? Am I fitting in as a guy? It doesn't stop until I go to sleep at night." Michael, a freshman at Towson (mentioned in the Introduction), feels the same gravity. "The hardest thing about being a guy," he told me, "is trying to beat the stigma on a daily basis."

This internalized pressure to embrace and to perpetuate static forms of masculinity is so great and constant it exacerbates at best, fuels at worst, the crisis of untreated anxiety and depression among young adults.

Michael spends many days "anxious, sad, lazy, and incompetent," he says, and therefore he doesn't follow through on most of his goals. Instead, he spends his time "playing video games, watching excessive television, and sleeping."

Zach knows all about this, too. The senior at Towson University tries to ignore these mental health problems because "they appear as excuses for falling short. As a man, it seems you are giving in to weakness if you hold depression and anxiety as reasons for not accomplishing goals."

He added, "There always seems to be pressure to 'man up and get it done' no matter what the task is."

Clearly, no one has taught or is teaching these young men how to negotiate the demands of a masculinity that keeps them paralyzed and miserable. Sadly, like most boys and men, they are expected to "know what to do when you don't know what to do" by virtue of their gender identity, as if that alone will—voilà!—lead to organic solutions. But everything about this identity—from the secretive shame and self-loathing of never stacking up to the fear of seeking help—prevents them from getting the traction they need to literally move on with their lives. It's the same lose-lose equation that mired Taylor in depression.

The thing is, many boys and young men do want permission to break out of this mire, as the Plan International USA survey showed. But the trappings of masculinity they feel forced to follow make the one arena of their lives where they could find emotional honesty and support off-limits: their male friendships. Few boys and young men have the life raft that Taylor and his friends created.

When I conducted focus groups at an all-boys high school, 32 percent of the nearly fifty students admitted that there are deeply personal things they would like to talk about but don't. The reasons? Approximately 27 percent of them said that they feel they should handle their problems on their own, and 33 percent believed that sharing feelings such as shame, humiliation, or sadness made them appear weak. When asked if they would want male friendships that included more listening to and support for their deeper struggles and problems, 48 percent said they would.

So do boys ever confide in anyone? They do and they will, but only up to a point. Psychologist Niobe Way has spent more than two decades researching boys of color in New York City public schools. In her book *Deep Secrets: Boys' Friendships and the Crisis of Connection*, Way chronicled how, up until the eleventh grade or so, many boys do maintain a close, emotionally honest, trusting friendship with a friend. That changes, however, the older boys get, the closer they get to manhood. In my own research, I discovered a similar dynamic but with a twist. Many older adolescent boys will maintain a close friendship, but, and this is important, they often establish fixed boundaries that mirror the friendship dynamics of older men.

Julian was an example of this. The high school junior from Baltimore would never talk with his parents about the things for which he most sought answers, especially when it came to social problems. Like every boy I spoke with, Julian had a group of several guys he hung out with, but only one he really opened up with. "I don't trust other people in our friend group to keep a secret," he said of his friends in his theater clique. Another reason he didn't consider reaching out to friends with questions or even to vent was because, in his words, he prefers "to take the brunt of the force initially. If I can handle something myself, it's better. It makes me stronger for the future. If I can internalize it, I can prepare for the future."

This is why many boys (many men, too) will reach out to a friend with what I call "targeted transparency." They seek out advice or solutions from a close friend who can help them navigate a specific area in which they feel in crisis—or "weak," as many of them called it. In other words, they won't create a fluid boundary with their male friends where they'll open up to each other daily or weekly; they've been taught that that would undermine their competency as men. They'll only go there with emotional honesty when they feel like they can't figure out something specific, essential, themselves.

The summer after tenth grade, Julian did reach out to a friend he trusted. After his girlfriend abruptly ended their relationship, Julian was devastated. He reached out to this particular friend because he had also experienced a breakup. Julian's friend offered some advice about how to negotiate this considerable blow, but what helped above all else, Julian said, was just knowing that "I wasn't going through it alone." That said, commiseration wasn't enough to help him stay afloat. Julian didn't use the word "devastated," nor would he admit to being severely depressed or suicidal. But he was all of those things. He couldn't bring himself to say them aloud, as if doing so would trigger them again. I know that he experienced these feelings because when I asked him if he had (with his permission, of course), he nodded each time. So, yes, he did sink into suicidal thoughts.

Adolescent boys, especially in high school, want their independence because they feel the need to prove their competency as grown men. While this quest for independence can be a good thing, moderation is essential. Boys who feel a deep, internal need to constantly prove their masculinity through independence don't suddenly realize the error of their ways once they become men. They don't suddenly realize, *Hey, I can dial back on this independence thing now that I've arrived and discovered the value of interdependency.* They become men who are too independent too much of the time—to their own detriment and to other people's—all in the name of proving that they're "men." They become men who hide their fear of asking for help behind a mask of hyperindependence, instead of seeking help.

Of all the boys I interviewed, Jonah was the most introverted, the most serious. In our one-on-one conversations and during my focus group with his class, Jonah intimated that he was at his private school because of an academic scholarship program geared toward boys of color from at-risk communities. He understood the opportunity and took it seriously. When he became "overheated" from the stress of school during sophomore year and was facing an emotional meltdown (something a lot of the boys I interviewed experienced), he reached out to his uncle, mother, and grandmother, who helped him understand that he needed to "open up more about my feelings, to vent." After that, he started looking for confidants—not among his family or male friends, but with girl friends. Jonah had a group of three guys he was friends with, but he turned to girls for "real support." The high school junior said that he appreciated the "solutions" and "advice" his male friends offered, but "sometimes I need to feel more supported, validated. And I can get it from my girl friends." He found that their "emotional support gives me more light and has made my relationships with other people better."

But Jonah also admitted that sharing his problems and feelings with his girl friends was a "blow" to his self-esteem.

Surprised by his response, I asked him why.

"I'm always afraid it makes me appear weak."

"But don't they want to help you?"

"I don't worry about feeling weak to them," he said. "I feel weak to myself."

Most of the boys I spoke with unintentionally revealed this inner dissonance when it came to their relationships with girls. On the one hand, they greatly valued and appreciated the chance to unload their emotional baggage. On the other hand, doing so slammed head-on into the ethos they had been taught about appearing invulnerable. To compound this further, boys like Jonah who already feel a degree of weakness sometimes wind up resenting women as they get older because the very thing they represent to these boys—vulnerability—is the perceived embodiment of femininity, something these boys cannot abide in themselves. These boys grow into men who resent women.

No one teetered along the tightrope between radically different spheres more than David, a senior with cerebral palsy. David was headed to an Atlantic Coast Conference college on a partial athletics scholarship as a student coach, a practice he honed as a team analyst for his high school football team and at NFL coaching workshops. Though he was close with a lot of the football players, David was limited by the "bro code," he told me. He didn't share his feelings with them unless "something really bad [happened]."

I asked if he wished the dynamic were different, if he could be more open emotionally. "Nah," he said. "It's all good. We get what we need from each other."

David expressed himself most with his friend Emily. His best friend since middle school, Emily single-handedly helped him navigate a "rocky" transition through middle school after his parents divorced and his grandfather passed away. From that relationship with Emily, David expanded his scope of intimate friendships to other girls. "They're just more caring, good at reading people's feelings, thoughts, and motives," he said. "I have a close guy friend, but he changes who he is, depending on who he's with. He tries to be cool to be accepted. Not girls. They're always themselves."

He said that once, after a party when a lot of guys had fallen asleep, David helped his closest male friend, the host, clean up. "Only then did he ask why I had had a 'sad boy' expression on my face all night," David said. Even though this friend had picked up on David's sadness much earlier during the party, he waited until they were alone to ask what was wrong.

Throughout our interview, David was all smiles. But when he started talking more deeply about his "bro" friendships, his smile disappeared. "Sometimes I feel things I wish my guy friends would pick up on."

What struck me during and after these interviews was how isolated so many of these boys seemed from each other. Many of them saved their deeper intimacies for friendships with girls, an all-too-common trend that many men continue for the rest of their lives. Beyond targeted transparency, these boys couldn't bring themselves to open up to male friends without fear of appearing incompetent or "weak." And even if they did open up, they rarely found the emotional support they sought, as David discovered from his closest male friend. The subtle threads of competition woven through and endemic to male relationships will inform their friendships well into adulthood.

During our interviews, I asked the boys if their school culture encouraged greater emotional transparency. "Sure," Jonah told me. "In advisory we talk about how to deal with stress." David spoke of the "amazing support" he'd always gotten because of his disability. But none of them were receiving or learning how to give the emotional support they so they desperately needed and, according to the 2018 Plan International USA study, so desperately wanted.

Where else are we, as a culture, going to sanction and encourage this if not in school? Where else will most boys learn about the powerful masculinity assumptions that limit them well into adulthood and about the importance of learning how to confide in each other and not only with girl friends? Shouldn't we start in the public setting where boys spend most of their time and where they need to learn healthy risk-taking?

———————

When I've asked teachers and administrators, especially at the high school level, how they get boys to talk about nonacademic topics, they inevitably boast about advisory sessions. These informal gatherings invite students to discuss sanctioned topics the faculty adviser hands down to them. Maybe they'll discuss drug and alcohol abuse, bullying, depression, stress. The one nod given directly to emotional intelligence focuses on learning empathy. While these topics are clearly important, I learned during my research that many of the adults don't feel comfortable, or even competent, leading the discussions. Or, more likely, it's not something they deem important in an academic setting. Either way, boys pick up on this overt devaluing of their deeper emotional lives—which squares perfectly with the messages they've received from early childhood. What's more, many boys perceive these group discussions the way that Sam does. The high school senior from Baltimore observed, "Most of the time we talk about things [teachers and administrators] want us to talk about. Even if these things are important, most guys could care less. It comes across as too preachy."

What do boys want to talk about if given the chance? Jeffrey Leiken, who runs mentoring programs and a boys' group at a Northern California school, said that adolescent boys want to know more about bravery and friendship, how to navigate relationships with girls, and how to garner respect from peers, parents, and teachers. "They want to talk about things that really matter at this stage of their lives," he told me. "They need to feel that their life really matters. That they're capable and needed in the world."

One of the few places where boys are given the time and space to explore their identity is the Sheridan School, a private K–8 school in Washington, DC. Once a week, six to twelve boys gather during lunch to ask the questions and vent the feelings that nag them most. I visited this group (to which Nico and Harrison, who appeared in the Introduction, belonged before moving on to high school) four times over the course of two academic years. During each visit, I was surprised by the growing sophistication of the discussions. Once, school Counselor and Boys' Group Adviser Phyllis Fagell had them take part in an exercise called the "man box." Calling out a series of feelings, Fagell asked the boys which ones belonged with masculine stereotypes. When the boys heard "trust," "sadness," "tenderness," "patience," "fear," "insecurity," "confusion," "feeling overwhelmed," and "joy," they all agreed that none of them belonged in the "box."

"You just eliminated eighty percent of human emotions from the male experience," said Fagell, who has written a book about mental health in middle schoolers. "Does that surprise you?"

They shook their heads.

"Wow, that's really impressive," she said. "You guys have figured out something that a lot of guys much older than you haven't."

"Well, we think about these things a lot, you know. This group has really helped us with that," said Harrison, then a seventh grader. A small sea of outstretched thumbs and pinkies wagged back and forth in the shaka, or "hang loose," surfing sign, which signals agreement at Sheridan.

As quick as they were with their insights about the "man box," one of them understood the gulf between knowing and practicing. "I'm still working on being able to express outside of this room, like, a quarter of what I express in here," admitted Nico in his Canadian Raising accent. Once again, hands were raised, thumbs pivoting as if turning pages in a new script.

The boys' group started as an affinity group when three sixth-grade boys drafted a proposal. At the time, they felt a bit embattled, Fagell told me, recalling how they were schooled in websites that renounced such hot-button issues as the gender wage gap. "Mostly I think it was in opposition to the girls in Fem [a female empowerment affinity group]," she said in a hushed tone. "There's a bit of typical middle school boy-girl competition going on there."

Much of that early resentment, however, has given way to creating something many of these boys realize is rare. "In here, we get to say stuff we wouldn't normally say in front of other people. And we *don't* judge each other," said a seventh grader with dark curls whose parents didn't want him to be named. "Boys should have a safe space to talk about things that matter to us."

This is no small thing, Leiken said. "Many boys want this. But they aren't given the safe space or the encouragement to do so in most schools." In my chats with this group, quite a few of them recalled pushback they've gotten from other boys outside of the group, from girls, and even from teachers when they've tried to talk more openly, with greater emotional honesty. When Harrison shared during a language arts discussion that he sometimes felt disempowered in school, his teacher fired back, "What are you talking about? You're a white male," he told me.

I asked some of the boys' group members if they supported feminism. They said they did . . . mostly. "I've always been on board with all of it," said Nico. "And I'm behind #metoo. But sometimes it feels as if boys have to be shut down in order for girls to speak up. That just feels unfair."

Two hundred and eighty miles away, Nigel struggles with this, too. The seventh grader at a charter school in Brooklyn is part of a LGBTQQ affinity group (the last "Q" stands for "questioning"). They have pushed for gender-neutral bathrooms, have initiated an anti-bullying campaign, and have spent "a lot of time" learning about toxic masculinity and lesbian and queer history. Nigel told me that there isn't "much space" to discuss the challenges boys face today. "There's not much boys can do or say that's acceptable," said the thirteen-year-old, who is still figuring out his gender identity. "There's just this constant pressure—we can't share our genuine emotions or feelings without being shamed from all sides."

Whenever he brings up these insights, he told me, the girls interrupt him or simply change the subject. He said that the female group members say that "they've had it worse for far longer. That's true. But it's not a competition about who has been discriminated the most." He added, "Shutting us down isn't righting any wrong. I just think it's really hard to be a boy today."

And boys always have to be wary about what they say, and how they say it, in the presence of other guys. "Boys get vilified if they say anything that comes out the wrong way or if it shows some degree of ignorance," Leiken said. "It becomes unsafe to speak out, and they shut down."

The focus of the Sheridan boys' group, and many of the ones popping up in middle and high schools nationally, isn't self-esteem. Just the opposite. If such groups are designed and managed deliberately, they can encourage "empathy and teach conflict resolution, collaboration, and tolerance," Leiken said. "This is about life skills development." These skills can translate into greater intimacy in their relationships and mental health. In his

2010 paper "Resistance to Ideals of Masculinity in Middle School Boys" presented to the American Psychological Association, psychologist Carlos Santos highlighted his study among 426 boys from racially and ethnically diverse backgrounds. Santos found that those who maintained closer relationships with their mothers acted less "tough" and stoic by the time they reached eighth grade. This resulted in closer intimacy with their friends and fewer cases of depression.

Much of the disconnect for boys in their relationships with friends and family boils down to a reduction of their identity, which often leads to emotional isolation. This begs the question: How can boys be authentic when we rob them of the language of their emotions? It was no surprise, then, when I heard many of the boys at Sheridan echo the sensation of "feeling alone" because of the thoughts and feelings they couldn't express without being "judged" or, worse, bullied. "This group pulls a lot of stress off my shoulders. This is the one place where I feel safe," Harrison said, a sentiment expressed by many of his Boys' Group peers. "I leave this group feeling better about being in school because I know that I'm not so alone about the things that worry me so much."

Parents, educators, and coaches I encountered in my research expressed the fear that when boys learn emotional authenticity they become too "soft" or "weak." But just the opposite occurs. Susan David, a psychologist at Harvard Medical School and author of the cutting-edge book *Emotional Agility*, told me that people who are the most resilient are the most emotionally honest and integrated. "People who suppress their emotions have poorer levels of mental health," David told me. "They have higher levels of anxiety and depression." And, she said, they're less authentic. The problem with traditional or normative forms of masculinity, according to David, is that they value a vastly limited range of emotions and, as a result, limited human experience. "All of our emotions, especially the ones we perceive as negative, contain signposts to things we care about—signals to our deeper values." So when we experience and allow ourselves to feel shame in an exchange with someone else, for instance, "real bravery and courage requires us to ask ourselves, 'Who do I want to be in this situation that will bring me closer to the interaction I really want to have with this person?'" said David. "It's about coming from a place of who you want to be in that situation. That's real authenticity."

———————

One of the few in-school programs that nudge boys to examine their inner signposts and to break free of static masculinity is called Becoming a Man, or BAM. The program, which is backed by a local research institution and managed and overseen by Youth Guidance, currently operates in 105 schools throughout Chicago and is slowly expanding its reach in large cities across the country. At present, BAM programs have expanded into ten schools in Boston and are getting a foothold in Los Angeles and Seattle. Youth Guidance has also developed a program for girls, WOW (Working on Womanhood). It's not a coincidence that the program operates in lower-income, high-stress environments that traditionally impact children's ability to flourish in school and that too often perpetuate risky masculine identities. To take a closer look at how BAM schools put into action the lessons that are having a profound impact on boys, I visited Wendell Phillips Academy on Chicago's South Side.

On a January morning when the temperature hovers at eight degrees Fahrenheit, I enter Wendell Phillips to meet Anthony Carpenter, the school's sole BAM counselor. The thirty-something Chicago native has a bushy beard, heavy-lidded eyes, and a broad smile and demeanor that are difficult to interpret as anything less than, well, a hug. He came to this job, in which he counsels and mentors six classes of high school boys (nearly seventy in total) every week, from a childhood of disconnect. "I didn't have a lot of friends growing up," he says. He remembers seeing Boys and Girls Club television commercials and thinking to himself, "I want to be part of that mentorship where someone tells me that I could be great," he told me. He found it—from the other side of the encouraging words—with BAM. The program, which is managed and overseen by the Chicago-based nonprofit organization, works with nearly 6,800 boys throughout the South Side in grades seven through twelve, helping them become more engaged in school, avoid nonviolent and violent behaviors that lead to arrest, and earn their diploma. Eighty-nine percent of BAM students attend school regularly, and 74 percent react far less aggressively after joining this program. BAM accomplishes all of this with a curriculum that requires boys meet as a class only once a week.

I notice how clean and clutter-free the hallways are. This is a school where anything that doesn't serve the express purpose of preparing these students to succeed in school and life doesn't make the cut for public consumption. Boys in the South Side miss an average of six to eight weeks of school per year, and it's not uncommon for many of them to read at a second- or third-grade level. The few posters and bulletin boards on the walls brandish examples of essays, lab reports, and résumés. The axioms that often are just window dressing in affluent schools serve a purpose here. In neighborhoods and school districts like this, they speak directly to the deep academic insecurity that is epidemic and endemic: "By failing to prepare, you are preparing to fail" and "It's not the finish line that matters; it's having the courage to start."

The BAM classroom follows the same protocol—a bare floor, a

collection of desk-chairs, a wall with chipped paint, and a military-straight row of posters that speak to such BAM core values as self-determination, accountability, respect for womanhood, positive anger expression, and visionary goal-setting. Above them all looms the school's grading scale. There are no computers or overhead screens. What's most noticeable to me is that the desk-chairs are all facing each other in a large circle. Anyone who knows anything about teaching boys knows that sitting in a circle is anathema to them. This speaks to a core sensibility; as with so many of the social dynamics in their lives, boys feel more comfortable sitting shoulder to shoulder. It's emotionally safer.

A musical reminder drifts through the hallway speakers, announcing that class will begin in five minutes. It's the theme song to *Jeopardy*. Eleven seniors file in and take seats amid the familiar soundtrack that celebrates, and mimics, the metronomic sound of cogitation. Carpenter opens the class with a BAM Check-In. The Check-In requires students to cycle through a brief inventory of where they "are"—PIES, they're called: their physical, intellectual, emotional, and spiritual states at the moment. On the surface, this seems like a tedious, awkward formality on the way to more substantive work—like having to introduce yourself at a workshop. It turns out to be just the opposite.

Carpenter begins by saying, "This is the Calm Lion checking in." (That's the nom de guerre he uses to kick-start some levity into the process, which is part of the counselors' job description.) "Physically, man, I'm tired. My wife and I have been sleep-training our baby." The deprivation registers on his face. "But all of this exhaustion with my baby is worth it," he says. "It's hard. But it slows my wife and me down and helps us keep our eyes on what's important. I have to tell y'all, slowin' down in my mind feels good. So, I guess that covers me for Intellectual, too."

BAM counselors pull double duty at Check-In. They need to call students out if they pony up superficial, one- or two-word responses, and they need to model the kinds of responses—read: transparency—they want to see in the guys. Carpenter just pulled off some fancy footwork. While he both shared and conflated two of his PIES, he also sent a subtle reminder about the need to think slowly. As with so many programs around the country that are teaching mindfulness meditation to at-risk children in urban school districts, nearly every aspect of BAM's curriculum, according to BAM founder and director Anthony Ramirez-Di Vittorio, seeks to teach boys that it's the "second thought that counts." This flies in the face of the "know what to do when you don't know what to do" mantra that shores up static masculinity.

The South Side neighborhoods these students live in are rife with homicide, gang violence, and crime, as well as a soundscape that is far louder for longer periods of time than that which more affluent urban dwellers experience. That is to say that the residents of these South Side neighborhoods are barraged with a constant stream of overwhelming, sometimes terrifying, stimuli that place them under siege. Neuroscientists have found that such around-the-clock trauma alters children's brains, impacting regions where learning, especially language acquisition and development, occurs. It also affects short-term memory and, as one special education teacher in Illinois was quoted saying, leaves children in a "constant, fear-activated state of hyper-awareness," which leads to quick rage as a means of self-protection. Children from these environments are often perceived as "defiant, disrespectful or overly aggressive," and it looks as if they're zoning out in the classroom, "but their brain is telling them, 'you need to be safe.'"

This is what led the University of Chicago Crime Lab, BAM's research partner, to the conclusion that, if any school-based "intervention" would make a difference, it absolutely needed to help boys with these areas: developing the skills necessary for emotional regulation, improving their recognition of other people's emotional states, figuring out how to work through their tensions with other people without responding reactively, mapping out goals, and developing "personal integrity." The Crime Lab's randomized controlled trial also suggested this panacea: teaching a "realistic, socially responsible view of adult masculinity to youth whose social environments often promote competing, more aggressive norms." Honestly, though, this sounds as if it could apply to practically any school in the country.

Ramirez-Di Vittorio and his partners at the Crime Lab have translated this research into a three-pronged approach for the BAM classroom: one-on-one mentoring, masculinity rites of passage, and cognitive-behavioral therapy techniques. BAM counselors—who also spend a lot of time working outside of class, mentoring students one-on-one—sit across from them, teaching and demonstrating such mindfulness practices as meditative breathing. Study after study shows the clear quantitative correlation between mindfulness meditation and far less reactivity, both cognitively and emotionally. As a result, students learn to think more clearly and for longer periods, and they learn to dodge impulsive words and actions that otherwise might lead to hostile confrontations. So far, BAM's evidence-based approach has decreased violent crime arrests among its students by 50 percent and has increased high school graduation rates by 19 percent.

As the guys take turns checking in, there's a trend with their "Intellectual" state. Nearly all of them say little about their academic situation. There are a lot of downward gazes, shifting around in seats, and refrains of "Yeah, I'm working on pulling up my F" in one class or another, followed by Carpenter repeating, "So, what's your plan for pulling yourself out of that?" This is met with shrugs and the occasional "Guess I need to get assignments in" or "Guess I should talk with my teacher." At one point, a student beams with obvious pride when he says that he pulled his F up to a C in English. Carpenter congratulates him and asks how he did it, glancing around the room, hoping the other guys are paying attention. "Honestly? I just spent more time studying and doing the work," the student says.

"Did y'all hear that?" Carpenter asks, locking eyes around the circle. "There's no magic to this. You just do the work. You've got this," he implores, gesticulating with his hands.

It's likely Carpenter sees himself in some of his students. "I always felt like there was something my peers had information about that I didn't," he told me. "So I never asked questions because I thought I should already know these things. I spent most of my time covering up what I thought I didn't know."

At first blush, it might be easy to dismiss what's going on here as typical adolescent male behavior—few words or feelings, visible discomfort—but that would be missing the deeper dynamic at play. For one thing, when they first enter into BAM—voluntarily, it's worth noting—a lot of the boys take a pass when they don't want to share, says Ramirez-Di Vittorio, who founded BAM in 2001 and taught these classes single-handedly for the first eight years of the program. What's also common, he says, are "a lot of one- or two-word responses like 'I'm cool' or 'I'm ah-iight,'" which dodge deeper transparency. Despite their obvious discomfort, these boys are owning up to their academic failures. And whether they act on the solutions posited or not, at least they are articulating and processing them as alternatives to the far more common tack for many males at this age, regardless of race or socioeconomic status: ignoring personal accountability and blaming their teachers.

On the BAM website, one graduate describes a small but sig-

_/

nificant breakthrough he experienced when the Check-In process finally paid dividends. During his senior year, he approached his teacher to hand in a project late. When informed that his project would only be eligible for a lower grade, he didn't "freak out" or call attention to himself at the teacher's desk, he says, which was his typical response. Instead, the young man accepted the teacher's decision calmly and respectfully. As an educator, I have seen this play out time and time again, so when this student described how he pivoted 180 degrees, I could hear the wheels churning through the muck of a paradigm shift. He told the teacher that it was his fault that he didn't turn it in on time and asked if there was anything else he could do to raise his grade. Had he gotten angry as he had so often in the past, he says, he would probably have been expelled "or my grade would have dropped even more."

———

When the BAM students share their Emotional slices of the PIES during Check-In, I'm reminded of what Ramirez-Di Vittorio said. As if they overheard what he told me, the barely audible refrains of "I'm cool" and "I'm ah-iight" skim across the silence. Anthony Carpenter isn't having it. "Now, y'all know the deal," he says, smiling. "You know I'm going to challenge you when you come up with responses that try to mask what you're feeling deep down."

Carpenter is met with a chorus of two-word, noncommittal responses, reinforced with heavy-lidded shrugs and seat shifting. The truth is, Check-In—in all of its apparently annoying focus on feelings and emotional transparency—is *the* draw for many BAM students. A 2016 report conducted by Chapin Hall at the University of Chicago found that students admitted that sharing their feelings wasn't the initial appeal of BAM, but that changed over time. Two-thirds admitted to eventually appreciating, even liking, the Check-In, and nearly half identified checking in or talking openly and honestly with their groups as the part of the program they liked most.

In this study, titled "Bolstering Belonging in BAM and Beyond," one student observed, "[Other teachers] don't do [Check-In] in every classroom. . . . In school, we don't get the chance to do that. We either bottle it up like I've always done, or we lash it out on other people and get in trouble for it. In BAM you get to talk about it and not get in trouble. You get to talk about it and actually get help, you know?" BAM students get to talk about what they "really feel," about what's "bothering" them. Another student spoke for many when he said that, at first, enrolling in BAM was a way to get out of some other academic course. But then he discovered the transformative power of expressing your feelings "without having people laugh at you." This was what prompted him to "stay in there": "having somebody to talk to about stuff that I wouldn't usually talk to people about." Perhaps this curt sentiment summed it up best from one student I spoke with: "The circle feels safe."

"We're teaching that it's okay to be emotional," says a counselor in the BAM report. "It doesn't make you weak, it doesn't make you a punk. It makes you real. It makes you honest. It makes you able to talk in a situation versus grabbing a gun."

Clearly, such profound emotional shifts, and, in turn, behavioral payoffs, are reason enough to see value. What many people don't realize is that when people feel more emotionally grounded and connected, their brains fire on more cylinders, and they buy into the learning process more readily. This is where programs like BAM intersect with social-emotional learning (SEL). According to the Collaborative for Academic, Social, and Emotional Learning (CASEL), SEL is a research-based program that teaches children (adults, too) the skills for, among other things, learning how to manage their emotions and feelings, showing empathy for others, and creating and maintaining positive relationships—all of which help with our short- and long-term goals and planning. The most comprehensive study of SEL programs in the US—a meta-analysis of over two hundred rigorous social-science studies—discovered these findings: students taught with carefully designed SEL curriculums scored an average of 11 percentile points higher than students who did not receive SEL training; they developed greater motivation to learn and a connection to school; they exhibited better classroom behavior; and they had improved attendance and graduation rates. There were big emotional payoffs, as well. SEL students experienced less depression, anxiety, stress, and social withdrawal. And, perhaps not surprisingly, they were less likely to disrupt class, to act out aggressively, and to receive disciplinary referrals.

Carpenter spends the rest of the class time teaching students about a new way to think of their anger—invoking the Jungian male archetypes of the constructive Warrior and the destructive Savage. This is the rites of passage work. He finishes off with a foundational activity that's part of the mortar-spreading and brick-laying, known in BAM circles as "group mission" work. Today, this consists of the guys standing up, facing each other in a circle, and dribbling a small orange ball upward in one hand and then tapping it to a group member. After a few attempts where everyone is silent and the ball barely makes it past the first guy, Carpenter asks them what they could do differently. "Hit it higher?" "Pass it around faster?" some boys ask. He tilts his head. His raised eyebrows and slight smirk indicate that they're off base. "Communicate!" a student with short dreadlocks calls out. Carpenter nods. Soon the guys are calling out each other's names as the ball remains aloft, making it farther around the circle.

Before class is over, Carpenter asks them for a brief Check-Out to see how they're feeling.

"Excited! I've got a lot of Warrior energy in me!"

"Happy."

"Determined."

"Patient."

"I feel more awake than at the beginning from the energy of this."

When it's the turn of one boy, whose slouchy posture and facial expression clearly broadcasted indifference during most of the class, he sits up and takes a few deep breaths. He has been holding the rubber ball, squeezing it while waiting his turn. "Sorry, but I gotta take it down a notch, fellas. Honestly? I don't want to be in school most days." He pauses and looks downward. "But I'm here because of you guys. I feel connected to you." He looks back up at the ball, now holding it with his hand out in front of him, palm upright, as if deciphering the future. "That makes me want to maybe stick it out. Try a little harder with my grades."

CHAPTER THREE

The Wiring of Masculinity—
The Ballsy Truth

There are times Chris struggles with his job as a nurse.

"I thought nursing was going to be about taking care of patients. Sometimes we act more like waiters and waitresses."

What bothers him most, however, six years into his career, is the "softness" of patients, especially the infirm men and women close to his age. "It's difficult when you have a patient in their twenties and thirties constantly complaining, 'My bed's too high' or 'Help me with the TV remote.' It's difficult to take care of people who are lazy."

Chris is thirty-five years old and lives in northeastern West Virginia. He enlisted in the army and eventually served eight years, including one tour in Iraq, an experience that absolutely colors his approach to work. When he encounters resistance and anxiety (read: fear) in patients whose lives are potentially in the balance, he tries, in his words, to be "stern without being blatantly mean. I tell them, 'You have to be able to take care of yourself, or you're going to die.'" During our telephone conversation, Chris never used the words "masculine" or "manly" or any derivatives of those terms to describe himself, his bedside manner, or how he wants the patients in his care to behave.

Still, these characteristics undeniably run through and run up against the constant demands and frequent frustrations of his job. He contrasts what he calls the "army-tough" mindset of pushing through extreme physical pain and suffering with the "lazy" patients who too quickly succumb to the fear of experiencing physical pain. "This behavior wasn't tolerated in the army," he says. "I have a different way of looking at things than maybe other nurses do. I've seen guys hit by an IED and have half his face blown off and still man his post, because that's his job."

Chris's attitude might not match the standard definition of a "compassionate" bedside manner, particularly for a nurse who has worked in both emergency and intensive-care units. But Chris, who grew up in western Maryland with dreams of being a doctor, really does want to tend to the sick. "Doctors may treat the illness, but nurses treat the patient," he says. "You see doctors on TV doing everything for patients, but in real life the doctor is there for a few minutes, and the nurse sticks around and does all of the work. We're the ones families see when a baby is born, and we're the ones they see when a parent dies. I like being there for my patients and their families at such times."

Many articles over the past few years describe men like Chris who are switching to nursing and other positions that historically have been considered pink-collar jobs, or "women's work," in the health-care, education, retail, and hospitality sectors. Many of these men didn't start out in these fields. But, in recent years, they have switched to them for a number of different reasons, most notably their need to find stable work and livable salaries in a proven growth industry. Such jobs are no longer in fields historically filled by men. "I was looking at getting into police work," Chris told me. "That way, I could still carry a gun and serve the country. Then I saw how police make so little money." A friend told him about the nursing program at the local college, its success at getting students placed in hospital jobs, and the bigger paycheck.

What few, if any, of these stories explore is the considerable extent to which these "new" careers require men like Chris—who grew up practicing traditional, sometimes hypermasculine, forms of masculinity—to confront their gender identity on the job.

When he started working in a hospital, Chris said he applied to nurse in the operating room. "The patients are unconscious, someone else deals with them, and you don't have much contact with patients or family members." Instead, he was placed in the medical surgery unit, where he cleaned and bathed patients and dispensed medication. "Passing pills for twelve hours makes for a long night," he said with a sigh. A month into this first position, he worked a night shift during which "three patients told me that I was a great nurse and thanked me profusely for being so kind."

To his surprise, the next day he took his name out of the running for the OR job.

Now a full-time nurse in an emergency room, Chris feels that his job aligns better with his own inner rhythm. "I'm not doing as much one-on-one. It's a faster pace. Patients are in and out. It's more adrenaline-pumping," he blurts out in a staccato, emphatic clip. And it's not just him. Eight of the ten male nurses at the hospital all work in emergency care.

As younger men like Chris continue to enter jobs that, for many of them, still carry the whiff of a "feminine" or "unmanly" skill set, we have to answer an important question: If men can perform work that supposedly goes against their nature, as some critics claim, are the sexes really wired all that differently, as so many people insist they are?

A nascent army of neuroscientists and researchers insists that the core physiological factors that have traditionally defined masculine identity—testosterone and the male brain—play far less of a role than we like to believe. While they do play a role, at the end of the day their influence is nowhere near as powerful as we've previously been taught.

———

The gospel of evolutionary biology has long informed our discussion about the roots of gender identity and our expectations about it. By now, we're well aware of the storyline—from our hunter-gatherer ancestors, males get the knack for spatial and eye-hand coordination skills; an innate compulsion to keep moving and remain vigilant, lest those saber-toothed tigers catch them; and a natural aptitude for constructing huts and traps.

Over the last two decades, some experts have clung tenaciously and vocally to these tenets, insisting that boys' and girls' brains are so different that the two sexes should be reared and educated differently. Such experts have maintained that testing-focused school classrooms undermine boys and their "natural" learning styles. Christina Hoff Sommers, a philosopher and ethicist, has beat this drum loudest, insisting that there's an all-out "war" against boys. In a 2013 *New York Times* op-ed, she wrote, "As our schools have become more feelings-centered, risk-averse, collaboration-oriented and sedentary, they have moved further and further from boys' characteristic sensibilities." Central to this argument is the belief that the old school "boys will be boys" sensibility continues to serve them, despite mounting evidence to the contrary.

In 2003, Cambridge neuro-luminary Simon Baron-Cohen wrote

a piece in the *Guardian* floating the idea—which he called the "empathizing-systemizing (E-S) theory"—that "the female brain is predominantly hard-wired for empathy, and that the male brain is predominantly hard-wired for understanding and building systems." Even today, more than fifteen years later, Baron-Cohen's theory continues to influence our understanding of gender and how men and women are supposed to behave.

Cordelia Fine is a psychologist and cognitive neuroscience researcher. She has written extensively about the intersection of gender and neurology, including in her book *Testosterone Rex: Unmaking the Myths of Our Gendered Minds*. The popular binary approach to gender identity championed by Baron-Cohen and others tests her patience. "How could our gender identities be so limited?" she wrote in an email to me. "We've undergone massive ecological, technological, social, medical and cultural changes through human history. Given that contemporary Western brains develop in very different conditions to those of our hunter-gatherer ancestors, why would we expect them to have developed [the same way]? This isn't the same as saying that we are 'blank slates,' it just takes seriously the many different developmental resources involved in brain development."

Fine is talking about neuroplasticity, the ability of the brain to change and reroute its synaptic sluices and connections based on changes in our behavior and in our environment. Neuroplasticity is the reason that people who meditate and practice mindfulness techniques can literally go from impulsive and hostile reactions to more patient, calm, thoughtful responses.

In addition to this synaptic shape-shifting, researchers are now finding that the supposed Mars-Venus chasm in male and female brains is actually a lot less significant than we once believed. Increasingly, neuro-research is finding that this tidy, two-system approach just doesn't hold up anymore. As editors from the *Scientific American* wrote in a special issue about the "New Science of Sex and Gender" in September 2017, "The emerging picture that denotes 'girlness' or 'boyness' reveals the involvement of complex gene networks—and the entire process appears to extend far beyond a specific moment six weeks after gestation when the gonads begin to form." In other words, our gender identities aren't limited by the in utero flood of testosterone that forms the testicles and penis. Case in point: researchers have discovered the chromosomal hallmarks of maleness, XY cells, in a ninety-four-year-old woman and a full-fledged womb in a seventy-year-old father of four.

While Fine duly acknowledges that there are some "average sex differences" in the human brain, she is quick to point out that "there are no simple links that can be drawn between a specific brain characteristic and a particular way of thinking or behaving."

When boys struggle with reading comprehension, for instance, it's not always because of their brain structure. Nor is this the reason why some girls continue to resist arithmetic. We often fall victim to the subtle "language" of our tribe—to the sanctioned social constructs. In other words, we're failing to succeed because our parents, teachers, and peers are telling us that we aren't naturally inclined to excel at such skills.

Now, this is *no small* statement. For decades, the binary brain crowd has highlighted the structural differences between the sexes. But recent research is dispelling these arguments. For instance, researchers were convinced that the reason girls find greater success in the classroom is because they have a wider corpus callosum, the bundle of white matter nerve tissue that connects the left and right parts of the brain. It turns out, though, the difference is negligible between boys and girls. Similarly, the amygdala, or the part of the brain that controls aggression, is not that much larger in males when overall brain sizes are compared between the sexes. In an email interview, Fine added that the gender gap in US standardized mean mathematical scores, long touted as evidence of men's natural left-brain superiority over women, has greatly closed. This reflects, Fine told me, "changed expectations, experiences, and opportunities" within society that are mirrored "at the neuronal level."

But it's not just math scores. Research shows that cognitive skills, including speaking and reading, and interpersonal qualities like aggression, empathy, and competitiveness are all heavily impacted by socialized norms. To find out if socialization really rivals the brain's innate circuitry, I spoke with Lise Eliot, associate professor of neuroscience at the Chicago Medical School of Rosalind Franklin University of Medicine and Science. "Each of these [brain] traits is massively amplified by the different sorts of practice, role models, and reinforcement that boys and girls are exposed to from birth onward," she told me. Eliot is the author of the critically acclaimed book *Pink Brain, Blue Brain: How Small Differences Grow into Troublesome Gaps and What We Can Do About It.* "Both women and men share a lot of the same instincts. This is what it boils down to—gender differences get larger with age, and this occurs, to a great extent, because of social segregation and socialization. In this culture, men and women live in such separate spheres where we're judged for our behavior."

Perhaps not surprisingly, these recent advances in neuroscience are ignored or dismissed within the scientific community because they contradict the perceived "natural order" of gender roles. How many of the researchers and authors who push binary brains have told us, for instance, the little-known fact that males and females share 99.8 percent of the same genes? How many have told us that baby boys are also attracted to human faces and baby girls to colorful mobiles, instead of consistently invoking Simon Baron-Cohen's oft-cited experiment that feeds into old binary notions? Harvard psychologist Elizabeth Spelke, who has studied infant cognition for decades, discovered that nearly all other research on infant attention to objects and human faces has parity in the infants' focus. Back in 1975, Stanford psychologist Eleanor Emmons Maccoby, hailed as one of the top psychologists of the twentieth century, and her longstanding colleague and partner Carol Nagy Jacklin dispelled many of the inaccurate gender "myths" that we still cling to today. In their book, *The Psychology of Sex Differences*, the coauthors observe that girls are not more social than boys; that both sexes are equally attentive to human faces; and that girls are not more "empathic" than boys. Maccoby and Jacklin insist that "the social judgment skills of men and boys have been seriously underrated."

Ultimately, Eliot drills down all of these layers of new findings into this takeaway: in the hundreds of imaging scans of both sexes she has poured over in her own research, she has found a pattern of "overwhelming similarity of deep structures and connections in the brain." Regardless of sexual identity, she says, our "subway map is the same." The 2015 study "Sex Beyond the Genitalia: The Human Brain Mosaic," published in the *Proceedings of the National Academy of Sciences of the United States of America* (PNAS), bears this out. Neuroscientist Daphna Joel and a team of thirteen international researchers examined the volume of gray and white matter in male and female brains in more than 1,400 brain scans from four data sets. While a "small group" of "sex/gender differences in brain structure" do exist, researchers determined that the human brain is ultimately neither female nor male. "Each brain is a unique mosaic of features" that are both male and female, the researchers wrote in their article. Between 23 and 53 percent of the brains examined in the data sets contained stereotypically male and female qualities or structures. But only up to 8 percent of these brains fell into the arch "male" or "female" categories. Lead researcher

Daphna Joel, professor of psychology and neuroscience at Tel Aviv University, underlined the study's key finding: "There is no one type of male or female brain."

When asked about studies conducted by neuroscientists that dispel her findings and insist upon inextricable ties between sex and wiring, Joel doesn't pull any punches. "There is no way to prove that these differences [in gender] have an innate basis, because the studies are conducted in adults," she says. "These are people who have lived their entire life in a highly gendered society."

While such findings surely hamstring many people with fear, ultimately they liberate both sexes and open the door to far greater possibilities in both the classroom and the workplace.

———

Begrudgingly, even some who disagree with Eliot, Fine, and Joel are getting on board with their findings—sort of. Leonard Sax, a psychologist and author who has long called for dramatic differences in the way we raise boys, acknowledges that a "third" type of brain exists, a neuronal mash-up of sex traits. And back in 2003, Baron-Cohen did suggest that a third or "balanced brain" seems to exist in some people. While some traditionalists are starting to cede ground, at least when it comes to the human brain, many continue to point to testosterone as the essence of what we consider "masculine."

One of the best examples I've witnessed of this played out when then-candidate Donald Trump appeared on the popular *Dr. Oz Show* just before the 2016 presidential election. Trump was touting the results of his most recent physical exam. The oddest moment of the interview came when Oz read aloud Trump's results, which Trump just happened to have in his suit pocket. Oz shared the candidate's numbers for many things, including blood pressure and the results of his prostate examination, electrocardiogram, and colonoscopy, all of which proved normal for any middle-aged or older man. When Oz said that Trump's testosterone level looked fine (it was 441, which is on the low-average side; 520+ is considered average), the crowd loudly applauded. Trump grinned and said how "crazy" it was that, when he played golf with Tom Brady, he felt the "same age as him." A lot of critics insisted that Trump, who is overweight and whose diet includes a lot of fast food, was needlessly, maybe even erroneously, touting his physical stamina. Personally, I don't have a problem with an older candidate wanting to show that he or she is up for the grueling demands of the job. What was more noteworthy to me was that Trump, an obsessive golfer, could have mentioned playing with anyone from the panoply of celebrities and professional athletes that he hits the links with nearly every weekend. This includes *professional golfers*. Yet Trump chose to mention Brady, a Hall of Fame–bound quarterback who plays in a league renowned for its hypermasculine brand of athletic dominance.

This barely concealed attempt at equating presidential fitness with hypermasculinity might seem over-the-top. But it's no different than the tens of thousands of guys on dating websites who post photographs of themselves with their shirts off or proudly holding a bigmouth bass or buck they just bagged, two culturally accepted ways to publicly display their masculinity and, subconsciously, show off their perceived virility.

More than even influencing the male physique and brain structure, testosterone is widely hailed as the reason why men are so hypersexual and aggressive; why they love taking risks; why they love to compete and strive to dominate. In nearly all cultures, testosterone is revered as the mystical subterranean spring from which "manhood" spurts forth. As far back as the twenty-first century BC, humans have known about the physiological potency of testosterone—and the lack of it. The ancient Sumerians were reportedly the first to intentionally castrate a man. Eunuchs, or men who had had their testes removed, developed and maintained less muscle mass. Their skin was softer, and their voices were higher. They had less body hair and, most crucially, a less threatening libido. This explains why, for thousands of years, eunuchs were prized for their roles as harem overseers and guardians of royal women. The ancients had no idea that testosterone was a naturally occurring chemical produced in the endocrine system that flooded bodies in utero and during puberty, the two most crucial stages of male development. They just knew that if you removed the testes from a man, the so-called "manliness" dissipated immediately.

The first formal experiment in what scientists call "behavioral endocrinology"—how humans or animals respond when their hormones are removed or manipulated—occurred in 1849 when a German physiologist named Arnold Berthold lopped off the testes of some roosters. Berthold observed that castration stopped the roosters from crowing. It also prevented the development of secondary sex characteristics, such as their large comb, and curtailed the roosters' aggressive behavior and desire to mate. Berthold then implanted the roosters' testicles back into their body cavities. Lo and behold, the mating, aggression, and crowing returned. Berthold was the first to realize that something in the testicles secreted an X factor into the bloodstream that impacted the male phenotype.

For all of testosterone's mythos, though, neuroscientists are discovering that it doesn't singularly command the spotlight when it comes to manly "success." It's a far more nuanced hormone that absolutely contributes to assertion and aggression—but its presence doesn't singularly drive these historically male behaviors. Contrary to what many of us want to believe, including many scientists and researchers, testosterone is not the "plenipotent executor of [natural] selection's demands," according to behavioral endocrinologist Richard Francis.

———

Justin Carré is a social psychologist at Nipissing University in Ontario. He studies the interplay between human neurology and the endocrine system and the way they influence competitive and aggressive behavior. Carré and his colleagues (Anne-Marie Iselin, Keith M. Welker, Ahmad R. Hariri, and Kenneth A. Dodge) launched a longitudinal ten-year study in four lower-socioeconomic regions around the country. They partnered with the Fast Track Project, which seeks to lower rates of violence and aggression and the resulting socially deviant behaviors that research finds are more likely in environments where emotional reactivity and violence are modeled for young children. The project and research were conducted in Durham, North Carolina; Nashville, Tennessee; Seattle, Washington; and a town in rural Pennsylvania. Children in the selected schools came from families where parents weren't monitoring and supervising them with much success or controlling their own aggressive outbreaks. As a result, the children in the study exhibited lower rates of emotional coping skills and lower academic skills. They also had poorer peer relations and regularly disrupted class.

These families were offered parent training sessions at home, which included guided parent-child interaction sessions. The children, most of whom were male, received skill training with academic courses, as well as with social peer interactions. Throughout middle and high school, these skills were augmented with courses and programs that helped with better decision-making, particularly in high-risk situations. When these boys reached the age of twenty-six, sixty-three of them participated in a follow-up experiment, which would measure levels of testosterone after a competitive game. The game was played between two males—either a Fast Track graduate with a confederate opponent, or a male who grew up in a similarly challenging environment without intervention and a confederate opponent. The goal of the game was to earn as many points as possible, which were later exchanged for money. Participants had three response options to the questions: Button 1 earned points after 100 consecutive presses, Button 2 stole points from the other male participant after 10 consecutive presses, and Button 3 protected points from theft after 10 consecutive presses.

Throughout the game, points were randomly stolen from participants. They were told that their opponent had taken them and were allowed to keep them. Participants were also told that, though they could steal points from their opponents, they were not allowed to keep them, rendering theft as "purely an act of reactive aggression," according to the coauthors in the *Journal of Psychological Science.*

What Carré and his four colleagues discovered was that the young men schooled in Fast Track demonstrated "decreased testosterone reactivity when exposed to social provocation." Conversely, high-risk boys not assigned to the Fast Track intervention demonstrated "increased testosterone reactivity as adults." The researchers deduced that early, sustained intervention programs that taught children how to modulate their emotional reactions to triggering situations influenced "the pattern of testosterone responses to provocation, which in turn influenced aggressive behavior." Baseline levels of testosterone had nothing to do with how hostilely these young men reacted during the game. For the first time, study authors claimed, research showed that learning how to modulate strong emotional reactions could decrease volatile reactivity that resulted from spikes in testosterone when men felt provoked.

Economist Amos Nadler and a team of six American and Canadian researchers expanded these findings in the article "Does Testosterone Impair Men's Cognitive Empathy? Evidence from Two Large-Scale Randomized Controlled Trials." Their 2019 study, published in the journal *Proceedings of the Royal Society B*, of two large-scale double-blind experiments in young men disproved previous research, which claimed a causal link between injected, elevated levels of testosterone and lower levels of empathy. Nadler and his colleagues observed that they found "no evidence that cognitive empathy is impaired" by the presence of higher levels of testosterone.

Why, then, do we insist on associating testosterone with aggressive, hypermasculine behavior?

Robert Sapolsky, a Stanford neurologist and primatologist, believes he is close to figuring this out. In his critically acclaimed collection of essays *The Trouble with Testosterone*, Sapolsky dismantles, in his trademark iconoclastic fashion, the commonly misinformed beliefs about testosterone and its historically loaded social and political implications. Dating back to the Sumerians, the assumption has always been that high levels of testosterone match up with high levels of aggression. But, according to Sapolsky, this isn't the case. Differences in testosterone levels—which some neurologists believe are regulated by the hypothalamus and amygdala—don't predict subsequent differences in aggressive behavior. "Similarly, fluctuations in testosterone levels within one individual over time do not predict subsequent changes in the levels of aggression in that one individual. . . . [G]et a hiccup in testosterone secretion one afternoon and that's not when [a] guy goes postal," says Sapolsky, who clearly enjoys a good turn of phrase. In other words, much as we might want to believe it, there is far less correlation between aggression and testosterone levels than we previously thought. What's more, testosterone levels aren't solely responsible for extreme aggression. Sapolsky says that if we castrated a man, then restored his testosterone level to only 20 percent of what it had been initially, then "amazingly, normal pre-castration levels of aggression come back."

Even if we were to inject the poor guy with twice the amount of testosterone that he had before, the level of aggressive behavior would return to pre-castration levels. To see any clear uptick in aggression, Sapolsky wrote, we'd have to quadruple the man's level of androgens, which is comparable to athletes using anabolic steroids. According to Sapolsky, a man's normal state of aggression will remain the same when it is sourcing anywhere from 20 percent of the original amount of testosterone to twice its normal range. "[T]he brain can't distinguish among this wide range of basically normal values," he said. This is why, even if we know the various levels of testosterone in a bunch of guys, it won't "help you much in figuring out who is going to be aggressive."

That's only half of the story.

Many of the hypothetical scenarios Sapolsky offers up in this book are drawn from research on both primates and humans. Take this one, for instance. Round up some male monkeys and let them sort out the social and dominance hierarchy. The monkey that falls in the middle of the pecking order follows the monkeys above him, dominating the lower ones. Sapolsky notes that this middle-range monkey will defer to the more aggressive monkeys with "shit-eating obsequiousness." But inject that middle-rung monkey with testosterone—enough "to grow antlers and a beard on every neuron in his brain"—and that monkey will probably become more aggressive. But it still won't be "raining aggressive terror on any and all in the group, frothing in an androgenic glaze of indiscriminate violence." He will become a "total bastard" to the monkeys beneath him, but, surprisingly, he will still kowtow to the more dominant monkeys higher up the chain. "This is critical," says Sapolsky. "Testosterone isn't *causing* aggression, it's *exaggerating* the aggression that's already there."

In other words, we've had it backward all along. Hormones like testosterone alone don't drive male aggression; social context, and how we respond to it, jacks it up or lowers it.

"Study after study has shown that when you examine testosterone levels when males are first placed together in a social group, testosterone levels predict nothing about who is going to be aggressive," Carré and his colleagues observed about humans. "The subsequent behavioral differences drive the hormonal changes, rather than the other way around."

In a 2018 paper, Carré and researcher John Archer wrote that there "is inconsistent evidence for a link between trait-level (i.e., baseline) testosterone and human aggression." Instead, a growing body of evidence suggests that acute changes in testosterone, viewed through the lens of "competition and/or social provocation," is a more relevant means for understanding "individual differences in human aggression." A good example of this is athletes who play contact sports. As we watch mixed martial arts cage fights, college and NFL football, professional wrestlers, and other hyperaggressive athletes, we often assume that their testosterone levels hover permanently at Olympian heights. It's true that many of these guys do have higher testosterone levels, but they don't maintain this level at all times. Many of the studies Carré and Archer reference in their paper have shown that athletes' testosterone levels rise and fall, depending on whether they win or lose, respectively. Research has also found this to be true with die-hard sports fans.

We see a similar pattern in that other arena where we roundly applaud unchecked competition in our culture: business.

It would be too easy to define the rapacious behavior of men who seek power and wealth solely as the result of greed. Of course they are motivated by greed. Beneath that, though, lies something else that rarely enters into the analysis: insecurity. In a paper that provides impressive breadth to this discussion, social psychologists Joseph A. Vandello and Jennifer K. Bosson observe that "men will often take measures to demonstrate or reestablish their manhood immediately after perceived threats to their gender."

In their lab at the University of South Florida, Vandello and Bosson focus on two types of risky behavior: aggression and financial risk. In one of their studies, they set out to see how men who felt some degree of threat to their masculine status would react to financial risk. Vandello and Bosson asked half of the male participants, who believed they were taking part in a marketing study, to apply a fruit-scented lotion to their hands. They asked the other half to "test" a power drill. Both groups then played a game for real money. According to Vandello and Bosson, the men who applied hand lotion placed "significantly larger bets" than the men who tested the power drill. "This suggests that financial risks may serve as effective manhood affirmations, especially after gender threats," they said. "The implications for the (strongly male-dominated) world of Wall Street are potentially far-ranging."

For decades, most researchers on the topic of men and risk-taking either downplayed or flat-out ignored the role of traditional masculine norms. Julie Nelson, an economist and professor at the University of Massachusetts Boston, isn't having any of this. She reviewed eighteen studies focused on men and risk-taking and found that "researchers often summarize results from earlier studies in an inaccurately stereotype-consistent way." She also found that their findings are consistent with the "stereotype of male risk takers, while downplaying (even sometimes to the extent of more or less ignoring) results that aren't [consistent with stereotypes]." In research circles, this is what's known as "confirmation bias."

The irony about all this testosterone talk is that it matters little to most men. It matters most to, and festers in the minds of, guys who obsess about their alpha dog status—the kinds of men Stanford sociologist Robb Willer wrote about in the *American Journal of Sociology*. Willer conducted a study that found that men with moderate to high testosterone levels were far more likely to "overcompensate" in words and behaviors when their masculinity was threatened, either overtly or implicitly. Compared with men who had lower basal levels of testosterone, they voiced their support for war and their contempt for homosexuality when the researcher said something they perceived as a challenge to their sense of traditional masculine norms, because they believed that saying such things would restore their masculine status. They strove to "pull their average level of masculinity up to more acceptable levels."

In *Testosterone Rex*, Cordelia Fine cites a study in which three groups of adult male participants were asked to play the part of father to one of those baby dolls that cry and sleep. Men in all three groups were told that they were playing the part of a husband who lets their partner handle most, if not all, of the childcare. One of the three groups was told to do nothing when the baby cried, while the second group was instructed to interact with the baby. What they didn't know was that this particular doll was reprogrammed to cry constantly, no matter what they did to pacify it. The third group received a doll that was programmed to stop crying when they provided the correct form of comfort. In the two groups that either ignored the crying baby or couldn't pacify it, the participants' testosterone levels rose. In the third group, their testosterone levels dropped once their efforts at consoling the crying baby hit their intended mark.

According to Fine, the discrepancy in testosterone levels in the crying baby experiment didn't occur because men with lower testosterone were more likely to be more nurturing. The gap occurred because "intimate caregiving itself lowered testosterone." Since the 1990s, research has found that couples in long-term relationships experience dips in their testosterone levels, and the big-rush neurotransmitters are replaced with the neurohormones oxytocin and vasopressin, which facilitate deeper emotional bonding. What's more, fathers who spend time caring for their infants and young children all have lower levels of testosterone. As their children get older, fathers' testosterone levels rise back up. But the larger point here is unmistakable: social and cultural situations dictate the rise and fall of testosterone, not nature and human biology on their own. The unexpected drop in testosterone that occurs during romantic commitments and childcare was designed to protect and perpetuate humanity.

This is something more fathers should keep in mind well beyond their sons' early childhood years. If more of them would continue to model compassion, empathy, and restraint when faced with vocal or physical provocation, male testosterone levels would remain at far safer and healthier levels for them and for the rest of us.

———————

I spoke with Chris, the nurse, a second time, a few weeks after our first conversation, and he sounded different. During our first conversation, his voice had a taut, reedy quality to it like a thinly stretched rubber band. This time, it came across like plant tendrils—looser, deeper, more splayed, rooted. I wouldn't have recognized that it was him, except for the graciousness that I had experienced earlier.

When we spoke this time about his experiences with nursing, things took on a different tenor. He seemed a bit more thoughtful and, I discovered, more transparent. I asked if working in nursing had changed him from his days in the army. "Back in my twenties,

I wouldn't have stood for half of the stuff I have to deal with now," he admitted, laughing. "I wouldn't have been able to wipe anybody's butt because of their incontinence, for starters. I would have told them to do it themselves."

But nursing has taught him tolerance borne out of context and suffering. "Sometimes I have older patients who can't control their bowel movements. They get embarrassed. They apologize, and I try to tell them, 'It's okay. It happens.' And I wipe them."

He said that nursing is connecting him to "who I was a long time ago, before I joined the military. I'm in the process of reversing back to who I was."

When I asked him what that meant, he said that nursing is making him "more caring and compassionate" by showing him sides to life he knew little about before (disability and chronic illness) and sides to death he never experienced in the army. "I'm trying to help people who are worn out and can't go on and want to cross over to the other side. I realize there's more to life than just life itself."

He still gets "incredibly frustrated and annoyed" by some patients and continues to practice tough love. A female patient kept removing an oxygen mask because it was uncomfortable, which infuriated Chris. "I told her that if she kept taking it off, she could die," he said. "I told her that it boiled down to this—either breathing or not breathing. After that she kept it on. Sometimes, not always, but sometimes, they realize that I'm someone who really is there for them."

There's a tension within Chris when it comes to his profession. Yes, he sometimes still wrestles with the image of nursing—old army buddies still chide him "all the time," he said, for "becoming a murse," a conflation of "man" and "nurse." "They ask me if I have to wear a white dress to work." But he never wavers in his commitment to his chosen profession, which requires from start to finish courage and resiliency and sometimes vulnerability. These are the characteristics that are defining modern masculinity more and more but still intimi-date other men. Chris's army friends, for example, continue to regard these traits as threats to his manhood or his perceived worth as a "red-blooded" American male. They do so at their own peril.

"Most of the guys who give me a hard time for my work are the ones still out of work, trying to figure out what they want to do with their lives," Chris said.

He wrestles with something deeper than the pushback from friends. When I spoke with him that second time, the softer, more thoughtful take on his work with patients butted heads with the more impatient, dismissive, army-tough tone that came through during our initial interview. I asked him if he aligns himself more with one camp over the other, with Army Chris or with Nurse Chris—the two identities that have, by his own admission, been at odds within him at times.

"I would like to think that I'm a balance of the two," he said. "Bru-tal honesty and deep compassion."

CHAPTER FOUR

Toxic Training

If you talk with most high school or college coaches or athletes, they'll describe their teams as "family." One coach explained this philosophy on a popular coaching blog: "Football is more than just a game, it's a bond, and it goes beyond the football field. I started using the #footballfamily hashtag a few years ago because football . . . provides a connection, a sense of belonging to a group."

A junior varsity football player at Damascus High School in Montgomery County, Maryland, proudly used that label, too, about his team. But that was before October 31, 2018, when he and three members of the junior varsity football team were attacked in the school's locker room, right before the start of the final practice of the season. The lights went out and, before the four freshman victims knew it, four sophomores jumped them and pinned them on the ground. The four sophomores then raped the four freshmen with a broom handle, plunging the stick against the boys' anuses through their underwear.

During the struggle, one boy had his underwear ripped off, and he was penetrated with the broom handle.

The incident, which was reported in *The Washington Post*, revealed that the sophomore perpetrators ganged up on the victims one at a time, while their teammates watched from outside the locker room, through a small window. One victim was held facedown over a bench and penetrated, while pleading, "Stop, stop, stop!" The assailants threw another freshman to the ground and tried to pull off his pants. When he resisted, the attackers punched and stomped him. Then they pulled down his underwear and raped him with the broom handle. All of the victims recalled afterward that their perpetrators were "laughing" the whole time and insisting that this was merely "hazing," a tradition the sophomore perpetrators had endured the season before.

What the sophomores endured, though, paled in comparison to what they had wrought; they ratcheted up the horror fivefold. Tragically, their willingness to escalate the violence was not unusual at all. It's part of a shocking national trend where victims become perpetrators and, like mass shooters who vie for the highest kill count, compete for an extreme form of cruelty that psychologists and many school administrators are still trying to comprehend.

After the incident, one victim said he couldn't shake the shame of his attack. Everyone at school, he said, knew he was "the kid who got the broom." Another victim described his life as shattered after he "was raped with a dirty broomstick in front of his teammates, by his own teammates." Other adolescent boys around the country who have experienced this form of sexual assault from their teammates—or "family" members—have been bullied for speaking out by other students and, remarkably, by more than a few teachers. In some cases, families have had to move away because the entire town had turned against them for threatening the reputation of a winning coach and football program. The incident report states that one of the Damascus victims told police "he thought the football team was supposed to be a family and look out for each other."

As horrifying as this incident was, it is by no means atypical. It reflects a growing shift in all of boys' sports—many girls' sports, too—where an already hypercompetitive culture has turned toxic. To date, most of the research on hazing focuses on the collegiate level, where a well-reported Alfred University study found that nearly 80 percent of student-athletes and members of fraternities and sororities experience hazing in some form. Research shows that 50 percent of college athletes first experienced hazing in high school, but that statistic overlooks the vast numbers of high school athletes who never compete at the college level. And, as some experts told me, this form of cruel sexual hazing is beginning as early as middle school.

Perhaps the biggest problem with all of this sports hazing is that its deeper values don't stop off the playing field. As we see time and time again, the toxicity beneath these so-called rites of passage bleed into the everyday lives of athletes who embrace this brand of hyper-masculinity, which literally affects every part of their lives, as well as the lives of the people in their communities.

———

What matters most in sports today isn't just winning. It's dominating an opponent. Nick Saban, one of the most vaunted, idolized, and quoted college football coaches of all time, is one of the many coaches who have normalized this mindset. High school coaches around the country tape the University of Alabama head coach's viral utterances to their locker room and office walls. A favorite was something Saban told his players before a game with Louisiana State

University, which has since become a popular online meme. "Dominate the guy you're playing against and make their asses quit." An online sportswriter for Alabama's sports website gushed over Saban's words, reminding readers that "humiliation is the object. . . . When [opponents] don't want to face one more second of humiliation, well, they'll do whatever it takes to get to 0:00 on the scoreboard and back on the team bus."

Among the many problems posed by this toxic mindset is that it creates a culture where humiliation and shame are the goal. As the chapter on violence points out, so much about dysfunctional masculinity centers around the paranoid need to shame the other guy before he can shame you. It's a prevailing mindset that has little use for sportsmanship or, most critically, for the humanity of the opponent facing you. It makes it too easy to ignore the batter you just hit with a fastball who's lying in the dirt. It makes it too easy to intimidate opponents with big hits that leave them motionless on the field. This wildly insecure and reckless mindset informs many types of bullying; it underpins the same warped thinking behind many of today's mass shooters; and it fuels the culture of misogyny that still targets women.

Ryan, an educator, administrator, and former football coach at a Virginia high school, grew up playing football and quickly found validation through it as early as middle school. "Football was this all-male thing," he told me. "It engaged me in a way that was powerful—it builds this closeness that feels authentic. You get this affirmation from peers, both female and male but more from males. That was always more important. It was a way that my father got affirmed by other men, and it was a way I did, too."

One of the things he loved most was the "immersive experience." Even at the junior level, every game felt like a major moment because everyone, from coaches and parents to students and teachers, was invested in the outcome, which made games feel more like pitched battles between two armies. "It's hard to recreate that in everyday life," he said.

Early on, Ryan played quarterback and loved the "authentic leadership opportunity" it gave him, elevating his status and confidence both on and off the field. Toward the end of high school, however, he became aware of something else about his chosen sport that jarred him. "As I got older, I realized that it taught a certain level of cruelty," he said. "Football teaches that the dominant man wins and that the dominant man is better. I went to church three times a week growing up and was always taught about compassion and Jesus turning the other cheek. Junior or senior year was when I realized there was a conflict there between church and what happened in the locker room and on the field." Ryan went on to play college football at a smaller Division I program, where he quickly became disenchanted with the "brutality" he observed daily. "Locker room fights started because of a mumbled slight. Power and dominance tainted every conversation. So much that was said about women was degrading. I lacked the courage and the context to say or do anything in the moment."

Another former high school football player spoke with critical candor in a controversial personal essay, which appeared on *Time* magazine's website in 2015. Like Ryan, Rian (different person but pronounced the same as "Ryan"), a doctoral student in communication studies, grew up in a football family. His father threw him passes or "routes" in his backyard, impressing upon his young son the need to "always come down with the ball," even if it meant a "terrifying hit from a defender." His older brother chased him around their childhood house, picking him up and throwing him down. "He was always trying to hit me hardest, so I'd be ready for the real thing someday," Rian wrote. Sports and pain were inextricable, and that was expected in his small Minnesota hometown where ice hockey and football predominated.

When we spoke, Rian recalled the first time he got hurt playing football. It was during middle school. As he ran with the ball, a defender tackled him. The hit pushed his shoulder pads up and pressed hard against his windpipe. Rian rose from the ground, his eyes filled with tears, gasping to breathe. His coach took one look at him and barked, "Fine! Get on the bench!" Rian said he had an "odd wheeze" in his throat for the next week.

During a tackling drill his freshman year of high school, Rian squared off against a large senior, a "nice enough guy outside of football" but who turned "agitated and mean" on the field. The senior hit Rian so hard his helmet popped halfway off his head, and his chin strap strangled his throat. He blacked out. A few seconds later, he came to, and the first thing he heard was his coach congratulating him on his toughness. After the season ended, he quit organized football.

At the beginning of the next school year, when the football season started, he stayed in his bedroom, ashamed for quitting a sport that he had so intimately tied to his identity. "I needed to process getting [physically] hurt, and that wasn't expected or allowed while I played."

In college, Rian reexamined his relationship to football. "So many guys play football just to show how tough you are," he told me. In his essay, Rian observed that his older brother, now in his thirties, still talks about the time he "broke the leg of the coach's son in a tackling drill. . . . I can see whenever he tells it that the story still carries a sense of achievement for him."

Jesse Steinfeldt has spent his career studying the intersection of traditional male gender norms and the behavior of coaches and athletes. The psychology professor and director of Indiana University's

Sport and Performance Training Practicum told me about a study that gauged how gender role conflict impacted athletes. Gender role conflict, a widely known concept in psychology, explores the negative, sometimes toxic, behavior that occurs when athletes think and play from a restrictive definition of their own masculinity. Contact sports like football and ice hockey rank highest on the gender role conflict scale. Steinfeldt told me that young men who played these sports were more likely to act out of instrumental aggression in pursuit of victory or on-field domination. At the same time, Steinfeldt found, athletes atop this scale are more likely to cheat and rely on unethical behavior to win. Lower down the scale were sports such as soccer and tennis. Steinfeldt said that his research has unequivocally shown that, "ultimately, gender role conflict comes from the coach who sets the climate for his team."

In this study, Steinfeldt and his colleagues concluded that "it is important that football coaches fully understand the impact they have" on setting the tone for their players when it comes to the use of aggression. This meant, wrote the researchers, that players learn how to use aggression responsibly and with constraints. Steinfeldt and his colleagues weren't calling for less aggression, or even violence, on the playing field. But they championed teaching young men how to "flip the switch," so that they could be "accountable and responsible young men off the field. . . . A football player who does not understand how to compartmentalize these behaviors may be likely to engage in antisocial behaviors (e.g., bullying, fighting) off the field as well," the authors wrote. They suggested that future research should explore how "sport-specific masculinity messages" about toughness and domination "might contribute to football players becoming conflicted" about "appropriate ways" to channel and limit their aggression to their sport only.

This was all well and good, I said to Steinfeldt, but how can we expect high school or even college athletes to do something as so-phisticated as compartmentalize the hyperaggression and domi-nating impulses they've been taught for years by coaches and often their own parents? What's more, the athletic field is *the* seminal place where many of these guys define themselves as both athletes and as men; as Ryan said, it's the sphere that matters most in their lives. Given all of this, I wondered, how can we expect them to turn off their reactive aggression and need to dominate once they walk off the field, when so much about the masculine identity they've been force-fed teaches them that it represents manly success?

"That's all true. It's very hard for these young guys," Steinfeldt admitted. "When we talk about compartmentalizing instrumental aggression, we're talking about an advanced level skill. Once that genie gets unleashed from the bottle for a lot of high school and even college athletes, it's hard to get it back in. These notions of courage and bravery they're taught can be warped."

This is something Ryan sees and wrestles with today as a varsity coach. "There's no two ways about it. Football has become a celebra-tion of big hits and dominance. You can't get away from it. And you can't live by those rules and not teach brutality and cruelty," he said. Given that most coaches imbue this ethos in their players, Ryan has come to believe that "football has limitations in terms of what it can teach boys about what it means to be a man. It's not enough. Sure, it can teach courage and sacrifice and loyalty for teammates. These do have real value, but they aren't enough in and of themselves."

After a long pause, Ryan added, "Since sports teach boys about life, we should also be teaching them skill sets they'll need both on and off the field. Empathy. Kindness. Thoughtfulness."

Rian agreed to this. "The reality for most boys and men is that you play football to appear tough. That's almost as big of an expecta-tion as the score at the end of the game. But football only has value if it's making better citizens, better fathers, better husbands. It should be teaching courage, for sure, but a different kind—the courage to do something you're uncomfortable with that serves and benefits other people. We shouldn't be teaching a brand of courage that celebrates brutality and dominance."

He's right—for reasons that exist far beyond the court or field. In her research, University of Pennsylvania professor emeritus of anthropology Peggy Sanday has found that tribal societies that are more tolerant of male dominance, rigid gender roles, and violence witness considerably higher rates of rape. In other words, apart from any potential biological predilection for sexual aggression, it flourishes and festers given the right cultural norms.

This is why sexual assault against women occurs more often on college campuses with high-profile and highly regarded sports programs. Typically, the perpetrators are athletes who play "power and performance sports," as sociologist Laura Finley calls them. Finley has written widely on the topic of school sports and violence, including sexual assault. She observes that student-athletes who participate in football, ice hockey, lacrosse, and wrestling, as well as in high-profile basketball programs, are the most common assailants. (Though male athletes who compete in lower-contact sports like swimming, tennis, track and field, and soccer are far less likely to commit sexual assault, they still do.) Her research, which corroborates with other studies, finds that nearly one-third of sexual assaults on college campuses are perpetrated by these athletes, which is nearly six times the rate of other peers. The only other male students who rival these athletes are members of the fraternities with the greatest social cachet: they commit 74 percent of sexual assaults against young women. Finley also found that these male athletes commit domestic violence in similar proportions.

Most of the research in this area focuses on the collegiate level, but a 2014 study set its sights on younger athletes. Researchers from the University of Pittsburgh, Johns Hopkins University, Harvard, and other universities canvased male student-athletes in sixteen Northern California high schools who had been in at least one relationship with a girl for more than one week. The boys were asked about their gender expectations in romantic relationships, and they were asked if they had physically, verbally, or sexually abused their dating partners during the previous three months. Of the 1,648 boys who participated in the study, 276 reported initiating some type of relationship abuse—physical, emotional, or psychological. Boys who believed in and practiced more "hypermasculine attitudes" were three times more likely to have recently abused their female dating partners. The boys who embraced the most hypermasculine attitudes played football or basketball.

Video games, which so many boys use for escape and entertainment, are perhaps the only place for these young men to find the power and affirmation they seek. They are designed in ways that appeal to boys and young men who don't always feel as if they fit in or can express their budding masculine identities around their more popular and more powerful peers. Like sports, gaming offers marginalized boys and young men a space to bond and to feel as if they are part of a community. A 2015 Pew Study, "Teens, Technology and Friendships," found that 84 percent of American teen boys play video games, and 57 percent of boys create new friendships through gaming. Many of the high school boys I interviewed confirmed that this is how they created and maintained friendships. Sure enough, the same Pew Study found that 88 percent of them talk while gaming, using a headset. This is a "major way boys talk with friends," the study found.

Boys and young men who seem to spend the most time gaming—and in chat rooms about gaming—are often males who are perceived as "nerdy," the ones who feel like pariahs in offline mainstream culture because they typically lack "gym bodies," athletic prowess, "cool" quotient, and sex appeal. In an ironic twist, rather than renouncing the hypermasculine behavior that often targets them, they lean into the parts of it that are still available to them and that have come to define gaming culture. And the results are exactly what you'd expect. Bonding through gaming often follows a hypermasculine protocol. These online friendships look eerily similar to what goes on in locker rooms—boys in a group turn on each other to boost their own status, and they especially pick on the most vulnerable player; they belittle him for his lack of prowess, all the while dismissing this taunting as the harmless cliché male rite of passage: "busting his chops." What's more, gaming appropriates a tactic common to the court and gridiron. The Pew study found that "older teen boys talked about how younger teens," in this case siblings, needed to learn how to handle "trash talk in games." When asked if younger boys couldn't just play these games without having to resort to combative language, one high school boy summed up the sentiments of many: "No, they have to do the same thing. It's for the game."

At the same time, recent research reveals that boys and young men are left with a residue of hostility and aggression after playing violent video games. Italian, American, and Dutch researchers are beginning to understand where this aggression is often directed. Their 2016 study, "Acting Like a Tough Guy," published in the scientific journal *PLOS ONE*, discovered a link between aggression against females and a lack of empathy that comes from playing violent video games. The researchers observed that "violent-sexist video games . . . reduce empathy for female violence victims, at least in the short-term. This reduction in empathy partly occurs because [these video games] . . . increase masculine beliefs, such as beliefs that 'real men' are tough, dominant, and aggressive. Our effects were especially pronounced among male participants who strongly identified with the misogynistic game characters."

Needless to say, the interrelated increase in aggression and decrease in empathy surely do not stop with girls and young women. Yes, video games are the most common way for most boys to bond. But it isn't a stretch to argue that alpha boys, the successful athletes and popular guys, surely target the less socially acceptable beta boys, who also are perceived as effeminate because they lack the dominant posturing the alphas have been conditioned to accept as their right.

In a discussion about toxic men in gaming for Polygon.com, Kate Miltner, a PhD journalism candidate whose research examines the crossroads of technology, identity, and power, observes that many boys and young men are "so intent on keeping technology as the purview of men. It's where they see themselves as having dominance and control."

Many girls and young women who game have spoken to this, lamenting the threats, sexual harassment, and endless stream of demeaning messages they receive from male players. While many male gamers treat each other with far more respect than they do their female counterparts, they still cling to the hypermasculine need to control and dominate each other.

A 2019 study published in the journal *Sex Roles*, "Video Game Playing and Beliefs About Masculinity Among Male and Female Emerging Adults," took this finding further. Researchers canvased 246 male and female gamers between the ages of eighteen and twenty-five. They found that when participants played violent video games, both males and females were more likely to condone hypermasculine beliefs about "aggression, dominance, and toughness, and the suppression of emotions." So, what do we take away from this? It's true that younger women are becoming more aggressive and are appropriating hypermasculine behaviors. Perhaps this research bears this out. But it's also worth examining the hypermasculine culture surrounding violent video games and how it can create a conformist zeitgeist that may work against girls' and young women's best interests and that they ignore at their own peril.

———————

It was a total Hail Mary pass. I had been conducting informal focus groups in a high school psychology class, speaking with juniors about their friendships. One all-male class had been reluctant—not just to open up about the degree of emotional honesty in their male friendships but to even approach the subject. Their facial expressions were the equivalent of crossed arms. Considering that they didn't know me, some random middle-aged guy, before I had walked into their Baltimore-area classroom that morning, I expected as much. Still, I knew that if anything beyond resistance was going to come from this focus group, I had to do more than ask them questions that clearly were making them uncomfortable.

That was when I told them about Brian and me.

During the first high school party I attended (in tenth grade), my new friend Scott introduced me to a neighborhood friend of his, Brian. Brian and I hit it off immediately. We started hanging out together on weekends after that. What drew me to him was the things he wanted to talk about and how he approached them. I had never had a guy friend with whom we both could confess our deeper worries, fears, and questions about the facets that defined our lives at fourteen or fifteen—demanding teachers, demanding coaches, finding our niches socially, and girls, the topic that held the most mystique and allure for us. Ounce for ounce, Brian matched me in his curiosity and insecurity, and we stayed up late most Saturday nights in our sleeping bags during sleepovers, purging the deeper fears and questions that felt smaller, less menacing, once they finally were exposed and illuminated in the darkness of his room.

"Do you ever feel like you don't fit in?" Brian asked one night. "You know, like maybe you don't belong anywhere, in any group?"

"Yeah," I admitted. "I've always felt that way. I can't stand hanging around guys who talk about sports and the things they claim they do with girls all of the time. So, that doesn't leave me with a lot of options."

"Man, it feels good to be able to talk about this kind of stuff," he said, emitting an audible sigh. "I can't talk about these things with anybody else. What about you?"

"Nope, I can't either."

Soon Brian and I started meeting up with a group on Friday nights, a mixing of guys we both knew from our respective junior highs. Those nights always took the same trajectory—skulking around the neighborhood where a lot of girls lived, ragging on each other, challenging each other to small acts of destruction and deviance, all of it committed for the larger purpose of screwing up the courage to eventually knock on some girl's bedroom window. Brian, Scott, and I were the only ones in the group who didn't antagonize anyone else. One Friday night, a kid Brian had been friends with for a long time, Brad, continually challenged Brian in front of all the other guys, daring him to flip off passing drivers or put some homeowner's trash can in the road. "C'mon, you wuss," Brad sneered. "For once, show that you've got a pair." Turning to the most popular boy in the group, Brad announced, "I've known him my whole life. He's always been a chickenshit."

A few minutes later, Brian told the group that his football coach had given him an award that week for courage during games. "Oh, sorry," he said to me, "I forgot that Andrew doesn't like talking football."

"What do you like talking about?" Brad asked. "Naked guys?"

Brian was the last one to stop laughing at this.

The next night I went to Brian's for a sleepover, and Brad was there for the night, too. I purposely said little, mostly because Brad spent a lot of time and energy ragging on Brian anytime he said something that could be construed as effeminate. Brian laughed off these insults, but they must have stung, given the late-night confessions we'd had in that same room. Before he turned out the lights in his bedroom, Brian egged on Brad to tell us about the tryst he had had recently. According to Brad, he had fooled around with one of the most popular girls in the grade at a party the week before.

"But you didn't just kiss her, right?" gushed Brian.

Brad leaned back on Brian's bed with his fingers interlaced behind his head and said, "Let's just say that my hand was in her panties a long time."

"You get her off?" Brian asked, breathlessly.

"What do you think?" Brad sneered.

"So, are you guys a couple?" Brian asked.

"Naw," Brad said, "she has horrible breath."

I didn't know why at the time, but so much about this moment made me feel squeamish and protective of some girl I didn't even know.

A week later, Brian invited me over to his house. When I got there, he and Brad were throwing a football back and forth on the front yard. Brian already had a plan for us—a game of one-on-one tackle football. Brad would act as all-time quarterback. This didn't bother me because even though I disliked talking a lot about sports, I always played them. But something made me uneasy in the way that Brian gave Brad a sidelong glance and smirk when he explained the game's rules. Brad looked down, kicking the dirt, and barely concealed his own smirk.

When Brian and I lined up against each other on the first play of the game, he looked up at me and said, "You're my adversary. It's an SAT word I learned this week. Adversary."

I must have looked confused (stunned was what I felt) because he asked if I knew what it meant. This was the first time any friend had referred to me this way. It felt as if Brian had sucker punched me in the gut.

"You're my adversary," he said again, smirking.

For the entire game, Brad's passes to me either soared over my head or skidded in front of me into the grass. On the last play of the game, Brad lofted high into the air a "buddy pass" intended for me. Ignorantly, I waited for it, and, just as I grasped the ball, Brian plowed into me. I laid on the ground surrounded by laughter in stereo.

Slowly, I picked myself up off the ground and retreated home.

Two evenings later, Brian called me on the telephone. He asked why I had left so abruptly. "If you don't know why, then I don't know what to tell you," I responded. He pivoted to the real reason for the call. There was a girl he liked, that he wanted to call and ask out, and he wanted to run his brief script by me.

Whatever he said was crowded out by my searing rage, and for some reason I didn't hear anything until this: "What if she says no? What if we do go out and she doesn't like me?"

Looking back, I don't think it was a coincidence that these angst-ridden questions yanked my consciousness back to the conversation. They created a space, a gap of raw trust, and I plowed headlong into it.

"What're you, a girl?" I literally spat, covering the phone in saliva. "You sound like some pathetic, whiny girl! 'Oh, what if she doesn't like me?'" I yelled in an affected female voice.

Brian hung up.

We never spoke again.

Within seconds of that phone call, my stomach roiled with toxic sludge. Not because I had hurt Brian's feelings. He had it coming. I felt toxic because I was so out of alignment with who I really was. This wasn't me. Even at fourteen, I never made fun of anyone for what they said or how they said it. I never thought boys should be criticized for being honest emotionally. Hell, I had been grateful for those sleepover nights when Brian and I did those deep dives together.

I did it because he had betrayed me. I wanted to wound him as badly or worse than he had wounded me. And on some level, I knew that comparing him to a girl would stop him dead in his tracks. At that moment, I was willing to betray everything I believed in just to put a dagger into his heart. To humiliate my friend.

What I hadn't realized when I shared this story with the focus group was how ubiquitous—how archetypal—it is in the male experience. Sadly, this is an anthem for most adolescent boys' (and, too often, older men's) relationships with other males. After I finished telling my story, I asked the class if they could identify with any parts of it. Every boy raised his hand.

In their book *Raising Cain: Protecting the Emotional Life of Boys*, authors Dan Kindlon and Michael Thompson mine the motivations and suffering of adolescent boys with striking clarity and depth. Their book is still the gold standard nearly twenty years after it was published. Thankfully, the coauthors avoid the trap of structuring the book around yet another simplistic "code" of boyhood or manhood and instead focus more on the complex socialized factors that shape, confuse, and beat down boys in their innocent quest to find their place. Kindlon and Thompson discuss the "Culture of Cruelty" that's pervasive among all boys, explaining how they "are loyal to its tenets" because it's viewed as an inescapable, "inevitable test of their manliness." In startling precision, Kindlon and Thompson sum up the fallout from this fealty: "With every lesson in dominance, fear, and betrayal, a boy is tutored away from trust, empathy, and relationship. . . . What they learn instead is emotional guardedness, the wariness with which so many men approach relationships for the rest of their lives."

This was what had motivated me to hit Brian where I knew it would wound him most—his fragile sense of "manliness."

Not nearly enough has been said about the role of competition in all of this. Few books about boys isolate competition as a factor in their problems, yet it looms large. Pachyderm large. When I interviewed CJ, a junior, his freckled, pale face flushed with fury when I brought up the topic. "It's the elephant in the room," he said. He set his jaw and narrowed his eyes. "You always have to find ways to come off as the better guy. You're always competing in a group of guys. If you're not doing that, then you're conforming to the preferences of the group, which are usually dictated by one or two guys." (He's right.) His anger grew palpable when he described how he practiced ballet four hours a week at a nearby all-girls school. "I can do superhero feats a lot of guys can't do like pick girls up over my head and throw them. But [at his all-boys school] guys see me as feminine." At morning assemblies, "guys pay attention and cheer when the lacrosse, soccer, or football teams win," he said, barely able to contain his anger. "But when someone mentions news about dance, theater, or some other recital, they talk over it or laugh."

Ultimately, CJ's identity was being ridiculed and ignored, which is enough to hurt anyone. But something else was also happening here. Despite his athletic prowess, CJ wasn't in the running with the other guys socially. His masculine identity wasn't being taken seriously, so he couldn't compete with them as equals, and he wanted to. "It's important not to get rid of competition because it can help guys push each other to be the best you can be," he said. "But not when it's used to put each other down and make one guy look better at another guy's expense."

Make no mistake. What CJ is talking about is a form of competition between guys—perhaps the least obvious and the most corrosive. Perhaps the biggest problem with the way we teach competition in this culture, especially among adolescent boys, is that boys' concrete brains cannot parse out its nuances. They cannot compartmentalize its reach, and they are encouraged to bring the same scorched-earth domination ethos to their careers, especially in business, and to their relationships with guy friends who, as males, represent yet more competition. It's an all-or-nothing affair. The only time boys are made aware of the dangers of competition is when they have taken it too far and someone else lies bloodied, literally and figuratively, at their feet.

———

Spend enough time at any sports awards banquet and, once you get past the cardboard chicken, you'll hear coach after coach rattle off the qualities they try to instill in their athletes: discipline, hard work, courage, teamwork, sacrifice . . . the list plows on. Ultimately, what many of these male coaches are doing—we've all heard this mantra time and time again—is "preparing boys for manhood." Few people, me included, would renounce the merits of these leadership qualities. Coaches know that virtually no one else is teaching boys about these characteristics, and they enter boys' lives at the perfect time to maximize their influence. From fourteen onward, many boys are like Rian, dreaming of ways to prove their manly mettle through sports. Even boys who outright reject this mindset a few years later embrace it during middle and high school, because they're ensnared in the web of conformity. Nothing bestows instant credibility in the eyes of boys like a public display of masculine behavior and aggression, particularly in guy-sanctioned settings like a rink, a basketball court, or the gridiron. Who better, then, to shepherd boys and young men into this highly coveted, if complicated, realm than coaches, who, by all accounts, hold the keys to this kingdom?

B. Elliot Hopkins, a former collegiate football player, told me a story that lines up with many other stories I heard when researching this chapter. "I spent more time with my [high school football] coach than I did with my dad," he said. "I can't tell you who any of my teachers were, but I remember my coaches, and I can tell you all that they said to us. I took it as bible."

When many ice hockey, football, and lacrosse coaches emphasize "toughness" in their players, they implicitly send a message to these boys and young men that this is what constitutes a man, perpetuating the Hobbesian worldview that life rewards brutality. Thankfully, a handful of nascent coaching programs are trying to change this corrosive culture. Coaching Boys into Men, a nonprofit organization with national reach, de-emphasizes a violent mindset on the field. Safe4Athletes advocates for the welfare of athletes when they fear they're being abused. And InSideOut Initiative is trying to change the "win at all costs" mantra through recreation-league and high-school-level coach training that places such old-school values as sportsmanship, life and leadership lessons, and fair play above winning and dominating.

Some of these programs are witnessing results that have profound implications beyond the court and field. A 2020 study published in *JAMA Pediatrics* analyzed the findings of a Coaching Boys into Men (CBIM) program in which coaches discussed gender equity, sexual violence, and the need to intervene when peers were being bullied. The study found that among the 973 male middle school athletes surveyed, many of them gained a better understanding as to what constituted abusive behavior, and some incidences of relationship abuse and sexual violence with girlfriends were reduced. The primary outcome: these adolescent males were more willing to intervene when they witnessed someone nearby being treated disrespectfully or threatened with physical harm.

Unfortunately, these programs have yet to capture the hearts or imagination of many high school and college coaches. For all of the viral internet stories out there about fathers painting nail polish on their daughter's fingers, many men still feel as if "masculinity" is under siege. When men who live by hypermasculine or even traditional masculine norms feel as if their behavior—their very existence—is under threat, they dig their heels in and all too often respond to this threat with aggression and violence.

Ryan, who played high school and college football, witnessed coaches and players turn on young men if they messed up during a game. "They called out your masculinity. The coach crushed us in the locker room. It wasn't uncommon for players to be called 'pussies' after losses or [told] that they needed to 'man up.' The worst were the film sessions of practices and games. If you made a mistake, it was rewound over and over. Then coaches would publicly humiliate you in front of your teammates. They considered this a form of motivation." Ultimately, Ryan came to this conclusion: "All of the power and dominance tainted everything—from the coaches and my teammates. Eventually, it overshadowed everything I had loved about the game."

Alex, a twenty-two-year-old former two-sport athlete in high school, endured similar experiences. Though he excelled in lacrosse and football, earning all-county accolades in both, he couldn't escape or excuse his coaches' abusive behavior. His football coach, who felt entitled because of his many state championships, regularly threatened his players, yelling during practices things like, "I will literally shit down your neck and skull-fuck you." When his players reacted with shock, he yelled, "I don't give a shit if they fine me for saying this."

As sadistic as his high school football coach was, Alex told me his lacrosse coaches were worse. His high school coach was young and cool and had played in college. He was everything Alex and his teammates wanted to be. He regularly bragged about his sexual exploits and asked his players about theirs. "We could talk with him like he was a buddy." When the players performed poorly during games, though, the coach "ripped into" them on a personal level. "He gave guys the silent treatment and wouldn't acknowledge them for a week. He would tell a teenager who struggled to play at a consistently high level, 'You can't be two people. We need you to be consistent— someone we can respect. Because we don't respect you when you play like this.'" Alex also witnessed him regularly shove his players.

When a lacrosse coach at a large public university in the Mid-Atlantic recruited him, Alex felt "really valued, appreciated. He made it seem as if we were kicking off this great relationship. Like a partnership." That sheen, of course, quickly faded. His college coach used a lot of the same psychologically manipulative tactics that his high school coach had used.

"If you're not doing what's expected," Alex said, "you're going to be treated like an outcast. If you aren't doing anything to win him games, he's doesn't show you any attention. He doesn't even acknowledge nonstarters." Then there was the way he chastised players if they underperformed, a familiar script of calling them "pussies" and telling them they needed to "man the fuck up."

The head coach practiced what Alex called "leadership through fear with consequences." Some of his veteran teammates told him about what the coach had done the year before he arrived. The team was practicing sluggishly. To wake them up, he ordered the players "to punch each other in the face."

A few years later, some of the underage lacrosse players received citations at area bars for drinking beer, and the coach found out about it. A week later, he called a 4:30 a.m. practice. He made players run for a half hour, then roll across the field. They had to perform one-legged dogs, hopping on one foot across the field, then log roll back. "I couldn't see straight, and I threw up for an hour and a half. Really, what was the point of that physical punishment? What did that teach us about responsibility or leadership? It didn't. We just wound up hating our coach for it."

The system failed off the field, as well. Injured and sick players were routinely shamed and judged by the trainer if he viewed them as "pussies" and not "sucking it up." The trainer dismissed Alex outright when he told him he felt sick. (A doctor's visit later revealed that he had strep throat.) Alex had quite a few teammates who had been kicked out of programs at other schools for behavioral problems that followed them to their next school. They weren't making the college transition off the field; they blew off classes and mandatory tutoring sessions and even missed team meetings. "They clearly struggled," he said. "But nothing was done to help them. The way you help these kids is by giving them the attention they need."

It wasn't until the end of his junior year that Alex and his teammates learned that mental health counseling services were available to them. "The coach had never told us, even though a lot of these guys needed it."

As I listened to Alex unpack all of this, I couldn't help but be reminded of soldiers who form tight bonds and camaraderie through the unimaginable stress, duress, and trauma they experience together. They fight more for each other than they do for anything else. Alex said as much. "We form a bond around dislike. You have to pick each other up, especially when you're going through something like this in the trenches together." His college career was nearly over when I interviewed Alex, and he said he was relieved. "I can't wait to be done with lacrosse. So much of what I've experienced and witnessed just shows me I will never do this to anyone if I ever coach."

From high school onward, he had experienced profound letdown, despair, disgust, and emotional scarring that had nothing to do with his abilities, his career, his injuries, or the game itself. Time and time again, the leadership styles of his coaches had single-handedly tainted the game—as it did for Ryan. "Look, I love the blue-collar attitude of hard work," Alex told me. "But at a certain point it's over-the-top. There's no balance here between being a lacrosse player and being a human being at the same time."

A 2005 study in the *Journal of Character Education*, "The Sport Behavior of Youth, Parents, and Coaches: The Good, the Bad, and the Ugly," found that 36 percent of adults who coached fifth through eighth graders admitted to yelling at players to motivate them. At the high school level, coaches flock to online discussion boards to vent about their athletes being "too sensitive," "too demanding," "too coddled," and unwilling or unable to "work hard enough." Worse, they resent the pushback from these boys—the challenges to their authority. During my research, I learned of a sign placed centrally in the boys' locker room at Columbia High School in New Jersey. It reads: "Losers assemble in small groups and complain about the coaches and other players. Winners assemble as a TEAM and find ways to win." This sign—which seeks to shame the adolescent boys for speaking out against their coaches—was erected after a lawsuit was brought against a baseball coach for making comments some of his student-athletes found sexist and vulgar. Many adults have no problem upbraiding their child's teacher (and principal) for something he or she said that was perceived as crossing a line in propriety.

Yet we don't hold coaches to the same degree of accountability. Sure, parents will complain if they think their child isn't getting enough playing time—just ask any high school or travel team coach about this. But parents *rarely*, if ever, complain about a coach's methods for what's perceived as teaching, guiding, motivating.

Why do we excuse this kind of behavior in so many coaches?

The most common reason is winning: the more a team wins, the more we *trust* a coach's process. Holding our index finger aloft when the scoreboard clock hits zero is so deeply ingrained in the American psyche that many of the people I interviewed for this chapter—from psychologists to anti-hazing experts—reflexively protected the hypercompetitive symbol before deconstructing it.

Beyond the largely invisible, deeply rooted influences on our competition consciousness, there are other reasons we don't question coaches of contact sports. Many parents, especially mothers, feel threatened when they have to negotiate hypermasculine coaches. Many fathers don't challenge these coaches because they fear appearing "soft" in front of these paragons of "manly" virtue who still hold the keys for men, even decades beyond their own adolescence. Perhaps this factor, more than any other, has the most resonance for parents: they don't question a coach's techniques because, even if deep down they don't trust this approach, they, too, succumb to the arm-twisting cultural ethos that developing into a man means learning how to toughen up and compete.

Tara Chaplin is a psychologist at George Mason University. In a 2005 study, she examined how parents responded to their children's emotions when they played a competitive board game together. What she and her colleagues soon discovered was that this dynamic revealed a difference in the way parents, most often fathers, treated the notion of competition between their sons and daughters. The research team conducted this experiment twice—when the children were four years old and again when they were six. They found that fathers reacted to their children more often and with more disapproval or approval than did mothers. When girls showed anger, the fathers ignored them. When boys showed "soft" emotions, such as sadness or rejection, the fathers ignored them. "It sent the message to boys that 'You're going to get ignored if you show sadness or anxiety when you're competing,'" Chaplin told me. "No child wants to be ignored. Fathers showed more emotion to girls when they showed submissive emotion, but they ignored boys if they showed that. They showed more attention to boys when they showed anger or disharmonious glee."

The interesting thing was that the children repeated emotional responses not because it made their fathers happy but because they elicited a response. Any response. "This was the weirdest thing," Chaplin said. "We initially thought what would matter to children was the type of attention they received. But it didn't. All that mattered was receiving attention. It mattered in terms of gender norms." For young girls, it sent the message to be compliant and amenable; to young boys, it sent the message to "go ahead and show anger or joy at dominating when you're competing," she explained. "It was basically a father's blessing or benediction to them to continue behaving this way during a competitive dynamic."

Fifteen years later, Chaplin is confident these findings still hold up. "I think that, in some ways, parents have changed, but we're still so ingrained in gender roles. Yes, we're trying to be more gender-neutral, some of us at least, but I think these messages from parents are still coming out."

———

Why do coaches push their athletes—of both genders—to the point of dehumanization? Many coaches—like many parents and bosses—

have long clung to the belief that negative motivation will yield the results they seek. It's true that instilling fear through the threat of violence produces the desired short-term results—scaring the athlete into focusing better or exerting himself more, for instance. But that payoff ends there, on the spot. It turns out that the longer-term dividends don't benefit him or anyone else down the road. If anything, they're toxic.

A team of researchers from the University of Texas at Austin and the University of Michigan conducted a study that explored the impact on children of open-handed spanking to see if this less severe form of corporal punishment really served its intended purpose. Their findings, published in the *Journal of Family Psychology*, advanced the large body of previous research: later in life, children who were spanked developed far more aggression and antisocial behavior; they struggled to control their behavior; they developed a less-fixed moral compass; their cognitive development was compromised; and they had a greater likelihood, not surprisingly, of developing mental health issues.

Trying to motivate anyone, regardless of age, to change his behavior or way of thinking by hitting him doesn't rewire neural synapses with the desired outcome. It doesn't even work when a child is verbally demeaned, intimidated, and beaten down, says Barbara Fredrickson, a psychologist and director of the Positive Emotions and Psychophysiology Laboratory at the University of North Carolina. Through her decades of research, she has found that actions and language that elicit positive emotions are the most effective way to inspire and lead. Her Broaden and Build Theory insists that positive emotions—feeling valued, appreciated, respected—play an essential role in our survival, prying open the mind and making it far more receptive to new ideas and creative ways of thinking and understanding. When people experience positive emotions, they are also more receptive to seeking out new resources and social relationships; this is the foundation for greater team building and bonding.

In a less productive team environment, teammates turn on and cannibalize each other, and sometimes they turn *to* each other, as they did on Alex's lacrosse team, to help their teammates endure the abusive treatment. Neither of these scenarios leads to greater athletic success or emotional, moral, or cognitive growth for anyone. Fredrickson, who also holds an appointment in UNC's business school, has found that when a person is faced with experiences that trigger negative emotions, including anxiety, fear, frustration, or anger, the mind perseverates on the perceived threat, which typically leads people to turn away from their resources and relationships. Highfunctioning sports teams—all relationships, actually—follow a ratio of three positive statements for every one negative remark. This is the ratio, research shows, where people achieve optimal levels of well-being and emotional-mental resilience.

A well-researched and well-analyzed *Sports Illustrated* article about the degree of abusive coaching at the college level revealed that this brand of positive psychology leadership barely exists, if at all. The National Collegiate Athletic Association (NCAA) conducted a study in 2010 called the Growth, Opportunities, Aspirations and Learning of Students in College (GOALS). The study canvased nearly 20,000 college athletes and found that many male and female athletes believed their coaches were often abusive. Despite coaches' sound bites conveying parental concern for their team, they didn't have the best interests of their athletes at heart, respondents insisted. This comes at great cost. Citing the ACHA assessment, journalists Alexander Wolff and Lauren Shute reported that 41 percent of athletes had "felt so depressed that it was difficult to function" and 52 percent had "felt overwhelming anxiety."

The article brings into focus the work of Bennett J. Tepper, chair of the Department of Management and Human Resources at Ohio State University's Fisher College of Business. The NCAA used the Abusive Supervision Scale he created (also called the Tepper Scale) in its GOALS report. An expert on workplace abuse, Tepper believes that the coach-athlete relationship mirrors the relationship between bosses and their employees, though, according to the article, abusive leadership is two to three times as prevalent in college sports as in the workplace.

When Tepper was asked whether notoriously abusive leaders in business and sports weren't wildly successful because of their old-school approach, he pointed to their brilliance in other areas. "The studies all say there's no incremental benefit to being hostile," he told the *Sports Illustrated* reporters, echoing Fredrickson. "Even when you control for a leader's experience and expertise, hostility always produces diminishing returns."

While hazing occurs on sports teams at the college level, it doesn't look anything like it does in high school—as the horrifying incident at Damascus High makes painfully clear. At the high school level, hazing takes on a form that's so surreal in its sexual violence and so difficult to comprehend that sports psychologists and hazing experts struggle to pinpoint just why it has become this way.

Over the past ten years, the mainstream press has started covering these incidents with greater frequency for the simple reason that more of them seem to be occurring and, importantly, are finally being reported to parents. On its website, ESPN lists incidences of hazing at the high school level since 1980. All of the incidents have this trait in common: they were committed by older athletes against younger teammates or sports camp members. The incidents include older athletes forcing younger teammates to drink or sit in urine, making them play nude games of Twister, whipping them with belts or ropes, and spreading feces on their bodies. In other reported incidents, older athletes forced younger teammates to race across a ball field with cookies (or some other food) wedged into their buttocks and to eat the cookies if they fell out. At other schools, these older boys hung their bare testicles on the faces of younger boys who were being held down, or they forced the younger boys' noses to press against the bare buttocks of an older teammate while doing sit-ups. The most violent of these incidents always revolved around some form of rape—older players forcing their fingers into younger athletes' anuses or sodomizing them with bottles or broom handles. At one school, a fifteen-year-old freshman wrestler was sodomized with a mop handle while teammates watched. The boy, bleeding and traumatized, spent a week in the hospital recovering from internal injuries.

His story is all too common.

One of the most glaring examples of violent hazing occurred during a summer football training camp at Reed-Custer High School in Braidwood, Illinois. On three different occasions, a fourteen-year-old incoming freshman was sexually assaulted. In an affidavit for the lawsuit, the victim said that during one incident four older football players attacked him while he was standing in line during practice. "The first guy who slapped me twice and knocked me down, he kicked me in my right side on to my ribs." Another player "took my shorts off and [the other perpetrators] pulled my legs up so that he could get his finger to my, you know, body part." The victim "yelled for help," "begged" for them to stop, and could "barely breathe." All of this occurred under the watch of the head football coach who, according to another lawsuit, motivated players before games to "unleash their inner rapist" and to "rip off" the genitalia of the opposing team.

At Navarro High School in La Vernia, Texas, between October 2016 and February 2017, a freshman on the basketball team was sexually assaulted more than thirty times. Over a three-year period, the perpetrators, who played on the varsity baseball, football, and basketball teams, targeted at least ten victims. They sodomized younger teammates with baseball bats, flashlights, and carbon-dioxide tanks. In an affidavit, victims insisted that school coaches "sanctioned these rituals," permitting a culture of hazing, and that other school officials "turned a blind eye toward the abuse, even after the abuse was reported to them." Coaches ignored the screams and cries of young athletes, and, in one incident, the basketball coach "observed" an assault with his team present.

An article in the online publication *The Daily Beast* quoted several mothers of boys on these teams who said that the sexual assaults became so routine that boys began wearing their underwear as protection in the showers—but to no avail. So many pairs of underwear were stuffed down drains that they clogged the plumbing. An Associated Press investigation examined nearly 17,000 reports of sexual assault committed by K–12 students over a four-year period. Sports settings emerged as the leading venue for such attacks.

B. Elliot Hopkins, a board member with Hazing Prevention and the director of sports, sanctioning, and educational services for the National Federation of State High School Associations (NFSHSA), told me that this form of "hazing" has "gotten far bigger than we ever thought it would be. It's criminal now. It's straight-out sexual assault." Susan Lipkins, a psychologist, author, and anti-hazing advocate who created and maintains a website called Inside Hazing: Understanding Hazardous Hazing, told me, "I don't understand how parents can send their boys into high school locker rooms today. It's insane that they'd want their kids to go play for a team and risk getting sodomized."

Hazing is nothing new. For millennia boys underwent rites of passage when they reached adolescence or puberty. These rituals often involved physical pain, suffering, and deprivation so severe that they sometimes left boys unconscious and purposely maimed in some degree. Among other reasons, the purpose behind this brutality was to prepare or "toughen" boys up for the rigors and demands of adult responsibilities in societies that relied upon hunting, gathering, and warfare.

In recent years, hazing has been distorted into something much more sexual and violent, something much more menacing and toxic. Boys ape their coaches, who indoctrinate them the only way they know how: through often violent acts they ignorantly believe will impart lessons about "manhood" and "brotherhood." They don't. "This kind of hazing is about power gratification," Lipkins told me.

Lipkins first became aware of this trend in 2003 when she learned about a boys' football camp on Long Island where younger boys were sodomized with golf balls covered in IcyHot, a burning topical pain reliever. Contrary to popular conception, this brand of hazing "isn't about sexual gratification," she said. The boys who do this—larger, stronger, and older than their younger, smaller victims—aren't sexually aroused in the same way that a child molester would be. "It's appealing because it's instant humiliation," Lipkins said. What quicker way is there to assert one's dominance than through humiliation? This is why rape with fingers or broom handles has become so prevalent.

As crazy as it sounds, neither the boys inflicting this suffering nor their coaches see this brand of "hazing" as rape. Hank Nuwer, a journalist, author, and anti-hazing advocate who maintains an exhaustive database of hazing incidents at the college level, said that this degree of suffering, humiliation, and the fear it engenders "elevates bully-type athletes in each other's eyes. They correlate this with toughness." Think of it as a rite of passage gone postapocalyptic. This was why one of the perpetrators in the Damascus High School sexual assault approached one of the boys he sodomized with a broom handle afterward and asked if the crying victim was okay.

This was why a distance runner with Olympian talent, who presently competes for a big Southeastern Conference university, was surprised when he and two successful wrestlers were expelled from their blue-chip Mid-Atlantic private school for participating in a small ring of upperclassmen who called themselves the Rape Squad. When school administrators discovered this ring and threatened serious consequences, the perpetrators didn't understand why. They said that the same thing had been done to them in the dorm years earlier and that it was merely "tradition."

How is it that this form of sexual assault is becoming so widespread beneath coaches' noses? Many of them sanction it. More and more of them are turning to their student team leaders to do their bidding with a generation that places most of its trust in peers. Lipkins told me about the captains of a soccer team at a university in upstate New York who are representative of this larger trend, which coaches argue is a way of empowering this peer-focused generation. They told her, "We're in charge of practices. How do we get the younger guys to listen to us? We haze them—it's a management technique."

Many coaches also perceive this form of sexual assault as little more than a "boys will be boys" tradition that encourages team bonding. This is why article after article cites lawsuits in which student-athletes insist that coaches knew about the sexual assaults and pretended not to see them or hear the screaming—as happened at both Reed-Custer and at Navarro. B. Elliot Hopkins told me about a lacrosse coach at an affluent public high school in Ohio who "sodomized his own player." When the coach was a high school athlete, "he was sodomized at this same school." Even though older coaches weren't sexually assaulted as young athletes, they believe in the value of hazing, regardless of its form—as a team-building epoxy and a rite of passage into manhood and the exclusivity of their team. As happens with child molesters and domestic violence offenders, "the victims of hazing often become the perpetrators," Lipkins explained. "It's all about repeating the tradition."

Though rarely discussed, one of the most common reasons coaches permit this form of "tradition" is because it speaks to the way men are taught and expected to process their suffering. In spheres where males have historically been forced to endure extreme deprivation, stress, and duress—military academies, post–medical school residencies—their traumatizing struggles are foremost hailed as a way to build resilience. It's lauded as "tradition" because this designation gives the men who have endured suffering the right to inflict their shame and psychic pain on younger, more vulnerable men. It's a sanctioned form of sadism, really, which perpetuates the deeply held belief that someone else must also pay when a man is forced to suffer.

Given all of these factors, it's no wonder that high-school-aged boys tolerate this barbaric form of domination because, developmentally, they crave belonging. Psychologists know this: both genders at this stage of life care more about fitting in and finding an identity that grants them status than anything else. "The perpetrators don't stop and judge [the sexual assault]," Lipkins said. "This is why I've even seen Eagle Scouts commit these acts. Kids who have good judgment leave all that on the sideline because they want to belong to their team, and we teach them to listen to coaches and team captains. Even though morality is probably there inherently for these kids, there's a different rule book when hazing enters the picture." What's more, the perpetrators get the green light from their coaches, and they see the hesitancy and utter lack of will from athletic directors and principals to label this a problem.

For all of the wonderful work many coaching organizations are doing with character-building and teaching boys about not carrying their aggression into their relationships with girls, little, if anything, is said about sexual assault against their own teammates. Lipkins said that when she gives talks to coaches or facilitates training with coaching organizations, "I ask how long they spend talking to their athletes about hazing. They say, 'Less than a minute,' because they don't value it. It's more important to them to teach how to win." Yet coaches wield unparalleled influence over boys and young men. "They're the ones who set the climate on a team and drive it downward."

B. Elliot Hopkins makes a similar point. "If coaches spent time talking to their athletes about this problem, hazing would drop off significantly," he told me. "If a coach starts the season by telling his players that they'll never get on the field if they [take part in this brand of hazing], everything would change. Think about it from the kid's perspective. You're gonna do whatever you need to do to be on the team and to get playing time." Part of the problem has to do with the way many of these coaches were socialized to embrace traditional, if not hypermasculine, gender norms. "Most of these guys don't feel comfortable having that conversation with their athletes," Hopkins said. "They can talk strategy all day long. But they're not trained for this."

The Associated Press article found that, in the aftermath of violent hazing, victims who openly challenged their coaches and principals spiraled into a disturbingly similar place: most of the boys became depressed. They had suicidal thoughts and sometimes impulses. They were bullied at school and on social media by other kids, who threatened to harm the victims and implored them to kill themselves—and sometimes even teachers contributed to the punishment. Often, the victims had to leave their schools permanently; sometimes the boys' families picked up and moved.

The mother of the victim at Reed-Custer was quoted for an online article: "I watched my kid go from a very happy, active, outgoing kid to a kid that stayed in his room, only playing Xbox, eating and being depressed. . . . He couldn't sleep because all he had running through his head were the people at school, where he was getting bullied and hazed. He had kids coming up saying, 'kill yourself,' he had kids coming to the lunchroom throwing barbecue sauce on him and I'd have to bring him a change of clothes. . . . I watched him go to a very dark place and I couldn't love him enough, care for him enough to help him out of it."

CHAPTER FIVE

Men and Vulnerability— A Crying Shame

As we walk across the quad, I am struck by the air. On this June evening in Norfolk, Massachusetts, the air is so dry I see detail in clouds—paint-brushed sweeps, swishes, and shading—that are uncommon in the muggy Mid-Atlantic where I'm from. This clarifying air seems to hold sway over the campus—from the echo of the crows overhead that ricochets off the large stone dormitory walls to the laughter and chatter of the men walking past in their starched white T-shirts and long blue gym shorts. I hear and see everything, as if microphones and speakers are hidden everywhere.

Despite the disarming beauty and serenity of this moment, I keep my guard up. I am visiting the Massachusetts Correctional Institution (MCI) Norfolk, the largest medium-security prison in the Massachusetts correctional system. Only minutes before, I had been waiting in a section where new prisoners are admitted with eight volunteers from the Jericho Circle Project. A new prisoner, a tan and muscular man who wouldn't have looked out of place in the nearby bars in Cape Cod, eyed me and, for a split second, leaned in my direction. I startled back, and the corrections officer yanked the prisoner back by his handcuffs, just in case. The exchange was innocent enough, but it reminded me of something Jericho Circle founder Steven Spitzer told me earlier that evening. "At any given time, one-third of these guys are lifers." If that wasn't enough of a reminder that I was visiting a prison, the eight volunteers and I had to follow Spitzer through a steel silo, then through a transitional area leading to the quad called the "Dead Zone," a gardened area monitored by rifle-toting corrections officers in watch towers.

I'm in prison to witness something that doesn't happen very much in the "real world": men talking about themselves and their lives with unflinching honesty—all in the presence of other men. They achieve this, from what I've read, through Jericho Circle, one of a small and growing number of programs in correctional facilities that encourage inmates to access a part of themselves that most of them abandoned long ago. For Spitzer, a former sociology academic who founded Jericho Circle twelve years ago, this means something unabashedly quixotic: "We're on a mission to help guys on the 'inside' find something that many of them lost or were never allowed to have. We're trying to help them flip the masculinity scripts they were handed at a young age."

An hour later, after navigating clearance in four different zones, we finally near the classrooms. I notice a library display featuring a string of novels and nonfiction books. They all contain the word "fatherhood" in their titles.

It's two days after Father's Day.

I follow Larry Cotton, another longtime Jericho Circle veteran, into the classroom. Cotton is one of fifteen "outside" men who volunteer at this prison. A retired structural engineer, Cotton has been meeting with these groups every week for ten years and resembles many of the older volunteers at Jericho: balding and paunchy, with a gauzy-eyed gentleness.

The men gather once a week, every Tuesday. The meeting I'm attending is the group's seventh of an eight-week cycle. Together, the fourteen men—seated in a circle at high school desks—have just completed the opening meditation. The inside guys are wearing white T-shirts, baggy gray cotton pants, and sneakers; I recognize quite a few pairs of white Reeboks. I have to admit, as grateful as I am to be here, sitting in a circle, facing these strangers—these inmates—makes me uncomfortable. I've worked very hard for a long time to break with the masculinity script and am all too aware that most hypermasculine men view sensitivity in other guys like a beer spilled on their shirt. Plus, I'm a guest, an outsider, and I'm more than a little concerned about upsetting the delicate balance they've established over the last six weeks. I know from having visited BAM in Chicago that the presence of a stranger can derail the willingness of these guys to do what they're here to do.

Like the boys at BAM, the men at Jericho are seated in a large circle. Spitzer modeled nearly every detail of the Jericho Circle— from the setup of the chairs to the curriculum—on the ManKind Project, an international nonprofit that facilitates weekend workshops and weekly meetings for nearly 10,000 men annually. The ManKind Project began in 1984 on the heels of the mythopoetic men's movement, and its mission and philosophy revolve around one geometric shape: the circle. The simple circle, it turns out, has had profound power across all cultures, dating back millennia. An archetypal symbol of wholeness, the circle represents the four seasons and the earth's four directional poles. Circles also have critical importance for the individual. In 1988, public television talk show luminary Bill Moyers interviewed comparative mythology scholar and author Joseph Campbell for a series about the power of mythology. Moyers, paraphrasing vanguard psychiatrist Carl Jung, said that "the circle is one of the great primordial images of mankind, that in considering the symbol of the circle, we are analyzing the self."

Campbell took the analysis a step further, recalling what a Pawnee chief shared with an American ethnographer at the beginning of the twentieth century. "When we pitch camp," Campbell paraphrased, "we pitch the camp in a circle. When we looked at the horizon, the horizon was in a circle. When the eagle builds a nest, the nest is in a circle." Campbell continued: "And then you read in Plato somewhere, the soul is a circle. I suppose the circle represents totality. Within the circle is one thing, it is encircled, it's enframed. That would be the spatial aspect, but the temporal aspect of the circle is, you leave, go somewhere and come back, the alpha and omega." In Campbell's seminal book, *The Hero with a Thousand Faces*, he lays this template over the timeless trials and travails of the hero's journey, placing the struggles all men face on the same universal circuit—departure, navigating life-changing ordeals, receiving spiritual aid, and returning "home." In this context, "home" means a man returning back to himself, more responsive to the needs of others, as well as to his own. This is why so many boys' and men's groups lean on the circle as they shepherd males through self-journeys many are too afraid to undertake on their own, let alone in the presence of other males who might judge them.

During Jericho sessions, the outside guys serve as observer-guides, while inside men facilitate them. An inside man named Jaime leads this group. He is stout and wears wire-frame glasses. As he talks, I realize that his tightly manicured salt-and-pepper hair and beard reflect his management style—clean and efficient, no wasted detail.

He is sitting beneath a large chalkboard, which is bordered at the top by the cursive and block letters of the alphabet, and a paper banner reading, "Vulnerability is the path and courage is the light." When the guys launch into the second stage of their sessions, they pivot to a check-in similar to BAM, except the men are expected to unpack why they feel a certain way. If they don't, Jaime "calls them out," pushing them to explore further. One inside guy, a white man in his late twenties or early thirties with a tightly trimmed beard and stubble on his nearly bald head, tells the group that he's happy, then tries to move on.

Impatient, Jaime barks, "You mentioned that you were feeling happiness—what's behind that?"

"I had a great workout today with my new friend," he says, turning and grinning at the guy next to him.

I am required to speak, too. Tentatively, I share frustrations and fears I've had about my marriage. At one point, I say, "You know how it is when you get really scared." Jaime cuts me off. "Now, hold on," he says, leaning forward and gesturing a stop motion with his hand. "Speak in 'I' statements. Not in second or third person. Remember, this is about taking responsibility for your own feelings."

One inside guy, who looks to be Hispanic or Latino and in his early thirties, talks about his "anger and sadness." His sadness, he told us, came from a phone call to his "ex" two days earlier. He called to speak with his young daughter, but his ex wouldn't allow it. "She's being vindictive," he said. "I know that I play a large part in why she feels this way, but she is still being vindictive. And it's—it's—" His voice wavers as he grows close to tears. Pushing through obvious emotion, he says, "It's unfair and wrong to implicate our daughter on Father's Day in all of this. And it hurt. Man, it really hurt."

I notice from the facial expressions on the guys waiting their turns that check-in isn't something that comes easily, even after seven weeks together. The legs on two of the inside guys are flapping like seagulls' wings. Yet every guy does his part. I notice an older African American man in his late fifties or early sixties—easily the oldest inmate in the group. When it's his turn to speak, he seems eager to share. He tells us that he feels "light." He explains that he moved to Massachusetts from Florida to escape the memory and legacy of accidentally shooting and killing his aunt when he was eight years old. "I loved my aunt," he tells us. "She was the most important person in my life, and I killed her." Silence. "Until I did the [Jericho Circle] Intensive last weekend, I've never told this to anyone," he continues. "Only my family knows. Now I'm telling you guys. And it's hard."

He looks down as he says this, then looks up again.

"But it feels good, really good, to finally let this out after so many years. Man, it's powerful to finally drag this secret out into daylight."

Before I entered the prison, a tall sixty-something volunteer named Jeff told me, "We call the circle 'building the container.' [It] can hold them and all of their trust, feelings, emotions, and hearts."

What's going on at Jericho Circle is complicated. For starters, it's part of a small, slow-growing trend in the American prison system across all levels of security, from low to high. It's also part of an emerging trend among men's groups and, in an organic way, among younger heterosexual men who are brazenly doing something we literally haven't seen since the age of Lincoln—saving much of their emotional intimacy for friendships with other guys. All across social media, young male actors, NBA players, and rappers now openly confess their struggles with anxiety and depression. Despite this common thread, this isn't an organized movement; it's utterly organic and splintered—and absolutely necessary. Publicly broadcasting vulnerability is an important step. But it's especially crucial that men learn to express this same vulnerability in front of other men—which is nothing short of revolutionary, considering how competitive males are taught to be in front of each other.

When I spoke with a small group of men in Frederick, Maryland, who meet once a week with their male therapist, many of them spoke about how this was the first and only time in their lives that they've been able to "practice being real with people," as one ball-capped man in his early forties said. "I've been able to have these kinds of conversations with past girlfriends but never anyone else." Another man in his thirties told me, "This is a space where you can practice figuring out yourself and what's deep inside of you. You can say or do anything in this group, I mean really fuck up, and still be forgiven. How often do guys get to do that?"

One of the most defining moments came when the group's co-therapist and co-facilitator, a boyish guy in his late thirties, spoke to how difficult it is for men to have these conversations with any therapist, let alone a man. "When I looked for a therapist for myself," he said, "I ruled out males. I didn't want to feel or appear weak in front of another male therapist."

This small but cresting wave of emotional transparency among men reveals a need for—and an awareness and acceptance of—men taking the risk and purging themselves of deeper struggles that make them appear vulnerable.

Some questions nag at me about this trend, though. For starters, why now? And why would these men take such a large risk when they surely know that doing so could have lasting, maybe even damaging, repercussions? After all, it isn't just a majority of men in this culture who have problems with other men appearing "soft." Many women do, too. And why are we convinced that men who show vulnerability are somehow *less competent* as "men"?

When we talk about vulnerability, we're talking about the most feared state or condition for most people. In a hypercompetitive culture like ours—where anything less than "winning" is dismissed at best or considered unforgivable at worst—vulnerability equals failure. In a rugged individualist culture like ours, vulnerability and the need for assistance equal weakness. As more and more women gain power and a foothold in traditionally male-dominated professions, this ethos increasingly affects both genders and manifests itself in a tacitly accepted form of protection against any whiff of vulnerability: the culture of perfection and, in turn, cool. In women, this translates into pressure with body image; with developing and balancing a successful career, social life, relationship, and perhaps children; and with just the "right" social media presence. Men today are just as caught up as women with this "perfect" or "cool" factor, which also means a focus on outward appearances—some of which intersect with, and some diverge from, the crutches women are using.

In this age of increasing anxiety over cracks in the foundations of so many of the cultural and institutional norms we have known up until now, men are doing what they have always done when they have felt vulnerable—leaning into traditional masculine identity. As always, their physical appearance is a reflection of the economy. They are frantic to muscle up their torsos and arms until they resemble NFL linebackers, obsessing about their waistlines, and covering their arms with tattoos, embodying the leaner, meaner era we live in. They are consuming more gangsta rap, more alcohol, and more extreme ways of being fans of such hypermasculine sports as NFL football, mixed martials arts, and NHL hockey. In other words, "cool" for men today (and for an increasing number of younger women) is about presenting an armor-plated presence to the world.

The reason we don't question, or gripe about, this embattled branding is because we tell ourselves that it conditions men, it makes them more mentally and emotionally tough for the challenges and expectations of manhood. But when people (up until recently, this had mostly meant men) swallow back feelings they perceive as "weak," such as sadness, shame, and fear, they do so at great cost. As Brené Brown, the author and scholar who has mined human vulnerability perhaps more deeply than anyone else, observed in a viral TED talk, "You can't numb those hard feelings without numbing the other affects, our emotions. You cannot selectively numb. So, when we numb [perceived negative feelings], we numb joy, we numb gratitude, we numb happiness. And then we are miserable, and we are looking for purpose and meaning, and then we feel vulnerable, so then we have a couple of beers and a banana nut muffin. And it becomes this dangerous cycle."

Brown has spent more than a dozen years researching what true emotional and mental strength and resiliency look like in humans. It always comes back to this: "We don't change, we don't grow, and we don't move forward without the work [of being vulnerable]," she writes in the book *The Gifts of Imperfection*. "If we really want to live a joyful, connected, and meaningful life, we must talk about the things that get in the way." Developing authenticity requires us to push beyond our deeper fears—which surface in the form of judgment and criticism of others—and to "cultivate the courage to be imperfect . . . to allow ourselves to be vulnerable," she writes.

This is what the inside men are doing through Jericho Circle. They are pushing beyond their deeper fear, shame, sadness, and guilt to find a deeper, previously verboten place of greater honesty and emotional authenticity. In a real sense, the men at MCI-Norfolk are pushing back against a prevailing norm that girds much of the American ethos. In the process, they are healing parts of themselves and fighting for more meaningful lives. "I have learned that

God doesn't make junk," one guy on the inside at MCI-Norfolk wrote in a testimonial. "I am a human being who has feelings and emotions. I have learned that life does not have to be filled with anger, rage, and pain. It is okay to feel good, [*sic*] it is okay to feel love." Brown, who openly confesses to fighting against becoming a more emotionally vulnerable person herself, says, "To believe that vulnerability is weakness is to believe that feeling is weakness." But accepting our deeper feelings and emotions, all of them, is what gives "purpose and meaning to living," she says.

There is nothing "cool" about what happens at MCI-Norfolk once the inside guys finish with the check-in and move on to clearing, the next stage of the program. This early stage in the two-hour-long session is where the inside facilitator, in this case Jaime, asks the group if they have any residual anger, resentment, frustration, or confusion over any interactions they've had since the last meeting. This could be tension with anyone—inside or outside. During my visit, only one inside guy indicates that he "needs clearing."

Jaime asks who he needs clearing with.

"Steve," he says.

"Steve who?"

"Steve Spitzer."

The guys in the circle look at each other, clearly baffled.

Steve Spitzer, the founder of Jericho Circle. The same Steve Spitzer who has spent the past twelve years recruiting and developing a network of volunteers to meet the growing demand for this program, which provides many of these men with a newfound sense of self-worth.

Following protocol, the guy enters the circle. He's the one who had the great workout with his new friend, the only guy in the circle who smiled during the check-in. His jaw is set and his eyes are riveted straight ahead. He spreads his legs and folds his hands over his lower abdomen and places his sinewy, tattoo-sleeved arms akimbo. He looks like so many young soldiers, cops, or martial arts hotshots whose barely restrained rage will snap at the slightest provocation.

Jaime asks the man's workout buddy to enter the circle as a stand-in for Steve. Jaime instructs the man to share his feelings with Stand-in Steve about the issue that concerns him. What we learn is that he is angry, "really pissed off," because the previous week Steve had told one of the inside guys in the circle that the gambling he confessed doing was against prison rules and could get him into trouble with prison administrators. The man points to the inside guy who had opened up about gambling. He then turns and tells Stand-in Steve, "What you said to him might have overstepped your role as an outside guy and could have huge repercussions on Circle gatherings."

Jaime then asks the man something interesting: "What feelings do you feel for Steve that you have mirrored yourself?" A sheepish smile crosses his face, and he shares a story about how he kept completely silent during his prison sentencing, despite entreaties from the judge and his lawyer to speak on his own behalf. "I refused to offer any answers for my crime," he admits, "which might have offered some answers, some clarity, for the people I hurt, including my parents and my own children. I was too proud and resentful." His voice becomes softer. "I remained silent, and for that I feel shame and regret."

Something has shifted, and it's not a stretch to say that Jaime's question hit its intended mark. Instead of animosity and retribution, the question encouraged compassion and empathy.

Next, Jaime asks the man how he would like to "move forward with Steve," and the man says that he would like closure. In the clearing process, the person with whom you are upset mirrors back your concerns and, in this instance, the man requests that the stand-in "apologize and take ownership." Stand-in Steve does both of these things, and the aggrieved man smiles. "I actually feel a little better, lighter," he says, then sits down.

But the mood of the room quickly shifts, as a noticeable gravity appears. A look of stricken recognition comes over the faces of many men, which darkens by the second. Now that he's out of character, Stand-in Steve looks particularly upset.

"Correct me if I'm wrong," he says to Jaime, "but gambling isn't one of the things we can be reported for by Jericho Circle outside guys."

More voices around the circle echo this, and they lean on Jaime for clarification. As it turns out, the dissenters are correct. Jaime tells them that an inside man can get reported if he admits to wanting to harm himself or another person; if he admits to wanting to do damage to the prison itself or the institution; or if he divulges information about an unsolved crime either he was part of or knows about.

"So, we can't get in trouble for saying that we gambled, right?" asks the older African American guy who shared that powerful story about his aunt.

Jaime nods slowly, his face blank, as if in a state of emotional suspension.

"You know," says Stand-in Steve, "when Steve said this last week it bothered me for a second, but then I let it go because I thought, hey, it was part of the contract we have with Jericho leaders. Now that I'm hearing that he threatened one of us for something that isn't part of our agreement, well, that infuriates me."

To my left, a guy with wire-framed oval glasses expresses his shock that Steve would "jeopardize everything we have worked so hard to create here."

My kidneys and shoulders seize. I need to be on guard.

Then the older African American gentleman erupts. "I share something I've never told anyone outside my family. And now I feel like I can't share nothin' anymore. All that trust is gone, man! Jericho Circle is bullshit!" he says, slamming his hand down on the desktop.

Then something unexpected happens. In a softer, almost child-like voice, he says, "How could he say that to us, knowing how hard all of this is?" He looks around the room at the ring of eyes—other male eyes—staring at him, and I wonder if the "container" seems to be shrinking in size to him, as it seems to me.

He stands up and yells, "I'm done with this, man!" and storms out of the room.

A call for Steve to appear ignites around the circle. Jaime tells the guys that they don't need him to be present, because he's in another circle and this is something they can work through together and broach with him another time. Clearly, Jaime is trying to do a few things here—de-escalate the tension and mounting fury; empower the guys to come to a temporary resolution themselves; and avoid what will surely devolve into a hanging jury, so to speak, at Steve's expense. But they won't have it. Any of it. Some of the guys are yelling that they won't work for resolution unless Steve appears. "We want Steve now!" bellows an African American guy with ink on his neck.

For the first time this evening, Larry Cotton, who has been helping facilitate these circles for twelve years, looks uneasy, unsure. Later, in the parking lot, he will tell me that nothing like this has ever happened before in Jericho Circle meetings. Right now, though, after witnessing how Jaime and the other guys are handling this conflict—far more productively than most men on the outside would handle it—I'm assuming that this kind of collective raw hurt erupts every session. There is no threat of violence from the kind of feelings that typically engender hostility in men, only men leaning into their deeper, honest fears and frustrations. One of the inside guys, who is white, built like a linebacker, and looks to be in his mid- to late twenties, speaks up. "How could Steve do this to us?" he asks, his voice cracking. He blinks fast to hold back tears.

———————

When it comes to displays of emotional honesty, perhaps no one action is more maligned and evokes more suspicion than does crying. We learn these reactions to crying very young, but they start out differently from where they wind up. Watch toddlers or even kindergartners when another child cries. Their eyes remain glued to the upset child, no doubt riveted in empathy and fear and dread at the thought of appearing that emotionally exposed themselves. Elementary school is typically when children first respond to another child's tears with the contempt for displays of vulnerability that many will harbor for the rest of their lives. This is when they begin calling children who openly weep "baby," a derisive commentary on the utter vulnerability and dependency of infants. At some point during elementary school, if children start conforming to traditional, socialized messages about gender identity, boys replace "baby" with another slur of repudiation: "girl."

We don't grow out of this shaming over a physiological response to pain, fear, grief, or sadness. If anything, it evolves into high art in cyberspace, where sharpened comments to online articles or social media posts impale male athletes, politicians, and celebrities anytime they tear up in public. Sure, some people come to the aid of the weepy, but most responses to tears in our culture are devoted to first scanning for ulterior motives. Research conducted by Penn State University psychologist Stephanie Shields and doctoral candidate Leah Warner, published in the book *Group Dynamics and Emotional Expression*, found that both genders' tears were generally acceptable—as long as they occurred in "extreme situations, such as the death of a loved one or a relationship break-up which the person is perceived to have no control over."

This is a topic that has come up in some shape or form every semester in my masculinity seminar. One of the first times it arose was in a student-created video. Toward the end of the semester, I ask students to undertake some form of informal research about a topic of masculinity that they would like to better understand. A female student orchestrated a simple but brilliant experiment: she filmed students coming and going between classes in the foyer of the crowded university library. In the foreground, maybe ten or fifteen feet away from the constant stream of students, she had a female friend sit on one of the large chairs placed there so the people walking past could see her. The young woman sat by herself, pretending to cry. Sometimes she sobbed. Many people, mostly young women, turned and looked at her, and a few young women even stopped to ask if she was okay. The next day, during the same crowded time, this student had a male friend sit in that chair and pretend to cry for the same amount of time. Three things were different in this scenario: not as many students looked in the direction of the crying male. Some people smirked. And no one stopped to console him or ask if he was okay. Nothing we read that semester captured as vividly as that video the subtle gender politics at play.

Two years ago, I conducted a survey among my undergraduate students and was surprised by the results. The survey gauged heterosexual female students' perceptions about their emotional connection in present or past romantic relationships with males. These surveys looked at such things as who liked to hold hands more often, who liked to cuddle more often, and if the women wanted parity when it came to sharing their deeper emotional lives. On many of these questions, the majority of female respondents said they did want parity. That dropped off precipitously, however, when it came to crying. Of the sixty-seven female respondents who identified as heterosexual, nearly all wanted the option to cry in front of their partners, but 49 percent found it "unattractive" if their partners cried in front of them.

It doesn't matter that recent studies have touted the myriad benefits of crying—from lower blood pressure to the physiological benefits that accompany stress and anxiety relief to a reflex that encourages greater selflessness and compassion. All of that flies out the window when many of us witness someone sobbing in public. It's true that some people react with compassion and empathy at this sight and attribute sincerity to the crier, as the research of Dutch psychologist and stress expert Ad Vingerhoets has pointed out about his compatriots. But many of us, especially in the US, react differently. Some wire trips in our amygdala, and we jump to puff-chested judgments about the crier because, deep down, the lens really isn't on others. We do this with most displays of vulnerability. This very human, yet unforgivable, state triggers such heightened animus in us because, in the perceived weakness that makes us squirm, we see the compromised person who scares us most: ourselves.

Most men never push themselves to turn the lens, and the light, on their deeper frailty. They refrain from this at their own peril. Steven, a twenty-eight-year-old who manages an insurance office in Eureka, California, shared with me his misery in his job, mostly because his boss is "abusive" and bullies him. "I spend Sunday nights crying." He once tried sharing his suffering with his parents, but their responses made him withdraw even further. "My father basically told me to suck it up until I find another job, and my mother didn't understand what I was going through." Even though Steven's parents encouraged him to reject normative masculinity as a child and to be like his father, a man who valued intelligence at the expense of sports, this gender-bending was highly selective. Displays of emotional honesty remained out-of-bounds.

Steven said that by thirteen he knew that he was depressed and needed help with his mental health. But he couldn't bring himself to tell his parents because he was expected to be "emotionally stable, to not complain, to be stoic." Well into his twenties, he "spent a lot of time weeping behind closed doors and sharing my sadness with strangers on the internet. I didn't want to burden anyone with my depression." Once he could afford to move out of his parents' home and had his own health insurance, he sought therapy. But he is far from healed, so buried and knotted are his feelings. "I was very bad at identifying my emotions in therapy, at first," he confessed. "We would have to work on describing my physical sensations and then name my emotions." He paused, before adding, "I'm embarrassed to say it, but I'm still slightly imprisoned by certain notions my parents taught me."

Will, a twenty-four-year-old educator on Maryland's Eastern Shore, had a similar experience, but venting his depression behind closed doors wasn't an option. His parents sent him to a boarding school in Virginia during high school, a place where students were expected to live up to the Spartan mascot ethos. "It was a suck-it-up kind of culture," he told me. "No weakness. You push through anything that didn't feel good."

We like to think that places such as Will's school don't exist anymore. But Phyllis Fagell knows otherwise. The counselor at the Sheridan School in Northwest Washington, DC, says, "I've definitely observed a double standard over the years. When it comes to boys expressing their emotions, male teachers are more likely to place a high value on stoicism. It comes from a well-intended place. I truly believe these men think they're helping a boy fit in when they coach him to 'tough it out.' And perhaps they are in the short term, but we know that boys who suppress their feelings will pay a price down the road. Several years ago, one of my eighth grade students was punched and kicked repeatedly in the face and back. As he sobbed, I tried to console him but let him cry. I still remember how a male administrator leaned over to me and said, 'He needs to pull it together and stop being such a pretty boy.'" This prejudice—and it is prejudice—is what makes it so hard to push back against overpowering norms, even among educators, such as this middle school administrator. It's the reason why participants in programs such as BAM and Jericho Circle are discovering and developing depths of courage and resiliency many men will never experience.

This mindset Fagell mentioned was rampant at Will's boarding school, where displays of perceived vulnerability, such as crying, were just cause for derision and being ostracized. This took a heavy toll on Will and his classmates. "There was a lot of underlying depression among the boys. There was a lot of anger and despair in the dorms." Will said that, during his junior year, one of his friends confessed to wanting to kill himself, but he was afraid of what it would do to his mother. "The administrators and faculty chalked it up to teenagers being moody. There was no discussion of mental health at all. You simply didn't talk about that sort of thing." During ninth grade, Will developed a serious case of depression, in part, he said, because his parents only reached out to him every two months with a phone call. He struggled to get out of bed most mornings, and on weekends he didn't want to see or talk with anyone.

I asked him why he didn't seek help from the school counselor.

"I didn't even know that there was a therapist. None of us did. None of the administrators or teachers ever talked about those kinds of resources for us. It wasn't a thing. We were supposed to behave like Spartans." So how did Will endure this muted suffering? "For a long time, I was a walking zombie. By sophomore year,

I decided that if I was going to get out of there, I had to submit to the culture of the school. At least in front of everyone else." This was a different story, though, when he was by himself. After football or lacrosse practices, he would "sneak out to a cow field nearby, stand there alone, and cry."

He did this several times a week, sometimes every day, when everything just felt too overwhelming. Even there, in that cow field removed from school, he couldn't escape the stigma of an emotional outpouring he couldn't control. "Crying felt wrongly relieving. It was something shameful, but it was something that I needed." It was probably the *one thing* that saved him, that kept him from running away—or worse. When Will graduated and went to college, he sought out mental health counseling. "That really helped me go through the storm of freshman year. It made a big difference. I just didn't realize how much I was hurting." Today, Will doesn't struggle with the same degree of depression, and he doesn't beat himself up when he does feel a need to cry. Well, not entirely. "I'd be lying if I said that I don't still struggle a little with crying. It still feels wrongly relieving. I'm working on getting over that."

Some men have not only come to peace with their emotional vulnerability but baldly embrace it and find a score of healthy payoffs from it. "I make no apology for my emotional reactions," Lee Martin, a novelist and short story writer, wrote in an essay about crying. "I say the hell with anyone in my life who told me while I was growing up that 'real men' don't cry. I'd rather be a crier than be the sort who never lets the world, with all its joy and sadness, touch him."

Martin told me that, from a very young age, he embraced this part of himself. It started when he was very young and lived with an aunt while his mother spent time away with his father, who was undergoing surgery and rehabilitation to attach prosthetic hands after a farming accident. When Martin's parents returned home, his mother allowed her young son to trust his vulnerability. A sensitive child, he would call for his mother from the dark of his bedroom. She always came. "She never complained, never tried to make me feel badly," he said. "She was just there for me when I needed her to be there. This taught me that it's okay to feel the things you feel, even if they're not the things other people think you should be feeling."

As a result, he told me, he learned to remain open to the helpful messages from adults in his life and to trust his instincts, which meant turning his back on the gang activity he was part of in his small, rural Indiana town—from the stealing to the drinking to the fighting, sometimes with knives. When a high school English teacher encouraged him to see where writing might take him, Martin listened. "I said to myself, I'm learning there are other ways to be a man—to give expression to my God-given talents. That was the year I quit basketball to devote time to writing and studies. I knew I wasn't the kid that everybody else was seeing." This also meant normalizing tears. "It's just a part of my life," he told me. "I'm not embarrassed by it or ashamed of it. If I weren't a writer, I think I'd still want to be engaged with the world—I think it's just a part of being human . . ." added Martin. Not surprisingly, this disposition gets mocked by *a lot* of men. Surprisingly, it also gets mocked by some women. For a while now, the internet has been full of memes, mugs, and T-shirts that lampoon this vulnerability with the sentiment "I bathe in male tears." Many feminists have dismissed it all as "irony" and that it's just an insider's joke, which as one website explained, makes fun of powerful "men who whine about how oppressed they are, how hard life is for them, while they still are privileged."

When I read this, I couldn't help but wonder if a similar sensibility informed the pushback that has plagued college-aged men in both the US and Canada who sought physical locations on their campuses so they could start men's groups—safe spaces to explore a different, more sensitizing masculine identity in the presence of other, like-minded males. These are young men who are simply trying to push back against norms that have shamed and traumatized them for far too long—and, as Martin said, that have limited their humanity. It's important to remember that privilege in no way diminishes the very real scars from emotional abuse and wholesale cultural rejection of one's identity.

———————

Eventually, Larry Cotton yields to the clamor for Jericho's founder. He pulls Steve from one of the six other meetings going on simultaneously, and Jaime explains the men's concern to Steve. "I'm sure it was just a simple misunderstanding," he says. "You didn't imply that anyone would get in trouble for gambling, right?"

Steve explains that, yes, gambling is against prison policy, and since Jericho is beholden to the institution's rules, then "we are obligated to report any trespasses if we want the program to stay in good standing with administrators. I wasn't saying that I was going to report anyone. I was just advising against such activity or against sharing it with the circle."

Jaime slaps his forehead, then his fingers slide up through his hair while he takes labored breaths. Seconds later, he leaves the room, slamming the door behind him. Later he will tell me, "In ten years of being part of Jericho Circle, I've never left the room during a meeting. But I was incredulous. He was compromising the sanctity of the circle with that threat. This was too fucking surreal for me to absorb. I had to leave."

In the vacuum of their leader's angry departure, something unexpected happens. Stand-in Steve wastes little time reminding Steve that gambling isn't one of the four big offenses and that he is out of touch. "It's becoming crystal clear that you're completely oblivious to the pressure we live with in this fishbowl twenty-four/seven," he tells Steve. "We have to constantly balance the realities of living in prison and all of its constant stressors and pressures with arbitrary, ridiculous rules."

The guy with the Civil War–style spectacles weighs in next. "Don't you understand that by threatening us for something that isn't against our four rules, it worries us that you or any of you guys on the outside might go behind our backs and tell on us for anything? Why would it just stop with gambling? Don't you see how, for us, this threatens the whole purpose of everything we've been creating with Jericho Circle? Why would we want to share anything if we can be reported for such trivial things?"

From the look of wide-eyed awareness on his face, Steve is clearly moved by their arguments and pleas. I can't speak for him, but I'm in awe of the men's commitment to communicating their needs with integrity and emotional honesty. Quite a few of the guys share with Steve how "hurt" they are by his threat. Whatever threat of mounting hostility or menace that existed up until Jaime's dramatic exit has been replaced with productive, emotionally restrained conversation, the kind that professional mediators urge for their clients.

At one point, a burly young white guy tentatively confesses to Steve, "I'm just having a really hard time here. I mean, you're supposed to be the guy with the answers. You started Jericho Circle. You're supposed to know better. I put you up on a pedestal." He looks even younger as his sad blue eyes widen and he looks down, burying his bearded chin in his chest.

"Don't you see?" says Steve, calmly. "You're defaulting to a Golden Clearing with me." Everyone looks confused, including me. "You're projecting onto me the very qualities you lack and want for yourself," Steve says.

As he says this, I look down and shake my head. Two inside guys across the room look over at me, and I hope that no one else has noticed. I don't want to be disrespectful, nor do I want to influence this process. Steve seemed so close to breaking through, and I was invested in seeing this happen, but now he's back in his head, coming from a place of defensiveness. He seems farther away from giving these guys what they want, what they need.

Sensing the growing frustration, fear, and need for affirmation, Larry speaks up for the first time. He says that he will "always protect your confidentiality, no matter what you share in this circle." This is met with applause. The bespectacled guy to my left then yells out, "Hey, I'd like to hear what the new guy thinks about all of this."

A bunch of the guys nod their heads, and a few shouts of "Yeah!" punctuate his request.

"It's really not my place," I say. "I'm just a visitor. I mean, I do have some thoughts about what's going down here, but they really aren't appropriate."

"Yes," Steve says, "share your thoughts on all of this. Your outside perspective might be helpful."

"Are you sure?" I ask.

Steve nods.

"Well, maybe, you know," I say, "maybe it might have helped for you to say to the guys, You know what? I fucked up big time, and I'm sorry."

Hoots and applause fill the room. Someone yells, "You just summed up what we've been feeling!"

Steve offers a partial smile and a lengthy explanation-apology, which includes two admissions that he "fucked up big time." He turns to Larry and says that the outside guys need to spend time with the guys in the circle, getting a better sense of their existence. "I underappreciated what you guys go through in here," Steve says to them, an admission that takes courage.

The session ends with all of the guys standing, shaking hands or hugging, and decompressing for a few moments. Jaime has returned and is giving bear hugs to the outside guys, including Steve. "Man," Jaime tells me. "Clearing has never lasted that long before or been that brutal."

On the walk out and across the quad, the evening sun is starting its descent in the early summer sky, igniting ethereal fireworks of pink here, peach there. Occasionally, the sun dips behind sharply defined cumulus clouds; initially, this leaves an impression of darkening in each cloud, but that dissipates and yields to utter illumination and transparency once the sun moves through it and beyond.

"That was a little rough in there for a bit," Steve says eventually. "It must have looked pretty dicey to an outsider." Above us a cloud turns opaque. "But that's okay. Because these inside guys are doing the hard work," he says as the cloud lightens and clarifies. "They're fighting to preserve and protect the one space in their lives where they can be their truest selves."

CHAPTER SIX

Men and Their Relationships— How to Fight Loneliness

The first time it happened, it was during the empty space, what Paul calls the "vacuum crisis."

One winter night about twelve years ago, the then-forty-eight-year-old was alone in his apartment, biding the hours between dinner and bedtime with his usual domestic chores, which distracted him from the struggles he'd endured over the past year. His chores helped keep his mind off something that had plagued him for much longer—four words that have haunted him since he was a child and left him feeling "fundamentally defective." All these years later, he could still hear his estranged father's voice, seething with disgust: "What's *wrong* with you?"

Whenever things had gone wrong for Paul—from his lonely childhood as a military brat to his brief career as a naval officer to the unraveling of his first marriage—his father's accusatory question fired deep within his neurological synapses and erupted full bore in his ears.

Before this night, though, he had never felt so hopeless, so lonely. What triggered him on this night, then? Paul doesn't remember, and given what he had been through, anything could have been the catalyst. A year earlier his second wife—who, he said, had abruptly quit their marital counseling and had unilaterally depleted their shared bank accounts—moved their three children four hours away. The lawyer had been so financially drained that he could only afford to board in an older woman's home. Moving into this one-bedroom apartment had been a slow climb upward.

He had been drinking heavily that night and crying, too.

"The first time I did this I felt so very empty," he said. "I really needed to have some kind of contact with another person. But how do you do that?" he asked me when we spoke. "There's no one you can call."

Paul did have three or four good friends from his undergraduate days at the Citadel whom he still spoke with regularly. While he could talk with them about the facts of his recent divorce, even his monetary woes, when it came to his deeper emotional life he couldn't get beyond the ethos that his military instructors had drilled into him: "Fuck it— just drive on." He couldn't bring himself to push back against his father's words raining down upon him: "Stop being so sensitive."

"There was always a tension inside of me," he said. "Growing up, I was really a sensitive person. I felt much more comfortable talking with my aunts, my grandmom, and my mom than with the males in my family. But, as I got older, I was taught that that was not how I was supposed to be."

On this particular evening, even excessive alcohol couldn't temporarily drown his fear of confronting these admittedly "ancient" and "dysfunctional" phantoms.

As Paul recalls it now, he still doesn't know why he did it.

"I hadn't planned it. Not in a million years would I ever have imagined doing something like this." Yet he succumbed to a compulsion that, all these years later, still leaves him wincing a tiny bit. Paul walked across his apartment to a spindly, floor-to-ceiling vertical beam near the dining room. "I wrapped my arms around that thing for all it was worth."

He doesn't know how long he hugged the beam. But he remembers, despite his drunken state, the revelation that shone through the miasma. "I remember thinking, Wow, this is actually working. I'm feeling a little better—and it's so fucking pathetic that it's working."

Over the next month, he hugged that beam as many as seven times. Why? Because it worked. "I needed some kind of contact—even if it was just something pressing back against me." Ultimately, he told me, hugging that beam "got down to a very basic need."

It was perhaps the first time he had allowed himself to admit that he was in need of deeper emotional connection. During one of the beam-hugging experiences, Paul thought, *This is so necessary and so pathetic, all at the same time. Where am I? What is going on with me as a person?*

When Paul felt the overpowering need to hug the beam again, he gave himself mini pep talks. "Yes, this is pathetic and weird," he told himself on these nights. "But no one else has to know about it, so it can only be so stigmatizing, right?"

The extremity of Paul's story lies in his act, not his despair.

In this one small yet defining act, Paul made himself vulnerable to *himself*, a subtle yet profound gesture Paul turned into a hinge moment. Had he suppressed the experience afterward and ignored it, nothing would have been gained. But he leaned into it, literally, over and over, and as a result he broke through to a place of reluctant acceptance about his desperate need for touch and affection, regardless of whether it was animate or not. "Just own it," he told himself during these brief hugging sessions. "For now, it helps."

Hugging the beam forced Paul to take a hard look at himself and surrender to his need for deeper, honest connection. "Interestingly," he told me, "things started to get a little better for me after this."

Before that fateful night twelve years ago, Paul behaved like a lot of men in his situation, drinking too much, working as late as possible, wallowing in all the ways that other people had let him down. When it came to his personal relationships—friendships, romances, and family—he was left staggered by the same two questions that haunt many men his age: Why is it harder to maintain these relationships than it was when I was younger? And why is it so hard to make new friends and romantic partnerships?

Unlike Paul, who slowly rebuilt his life, many men never get beyond these questions. They stay stuck in the mindset that their platonic and romantic relationships either work or they don't. Research now undeniably shows, however, that this all too common script, which discourages introspection and a work ethic aimed at relationships, doesn't serve them in the long run. It sets many guys up for a lifetime of emotional isolation that leads to disastrous long-term effects, both for them and for the people in their lives.

———

The kind of emotional isolation Paul experienced isn't rare or even new, and it can impact our health. More than two hundred studies worldwide, involving more than three million individuals, have found that loneliness is more toxic to our long-term health than cigarettes or obesity. Like a carcinogen, loneliness puts us at greater risk for heart disease, stroke, certain cancers, and immune system impairment, not to mention a number of mental illnesses, from dementia and depression to chronic anxiety. Robert Putnam examined the effects of emotional isolation in his 2000 book *Bowling Alone*, which explores our decreasing desire to create and maintain social capital (extending ourselves to strangers without expecting anything in return), a core, disturbing trend that has accelerated since the early 1970s. Sociologist David Riesman was the first to chronicle this trend in his seminal book, *The Lonely Crowd*. He observed in 1950 that the ascendancy of post–World War II consumerism and corporations turned Americans' focus outward, or "other-directed," causing us to base our sense of self on other people's perceptions of us. His words proved to be eerily prescient: "The other-directed person wants to be loved rather than esteemed." That is, people who spend a lot of time seeking validation from others—which is taken to new heights in this nascent age of social media—equate this "fitting in" with a form of love on some deeper level. They consider being connected and accepted the same as being loved, even when it's validation from acquaintances and virtual strangers.

For many men, this means seeking the approval of other men they admire through hypermasculine behavior that reaffirms their perceived status as worthy men. A 2006 report chronicling "changes in core discussion networks over two decades," found that over a twenty-year period the number of friends in whom Americans confide has shrunk as much as 33 percent. More specifically, the report found that the number of close friends for many adults had decreased from 3.5 in the 1980s to 2 in 2004. While American social scientists have been studying social isolation within this culture for decades, their research still has a blind spot. Little of it has focused on the epidemic hitting men hardest. Many researchers, such as Julianne Holt-Lunstad, have blithely maintained that both genders suffer equally from the plague of loneliness. Initially, that might appear to be true, because women check off this box in studies in far greater numbers than men. But other studies dating as far back as the 1980s—which rely on such gold-standard diagnostic yardsticks as the UCLA Loneliness Scale—have argued otherwise. This helps explain why research conducted with 4,130 German singles found that single men were lonelier than single women, who are happier, less lonely, and more psychologically balanced. A recent report conducted by UK-based Samaritans vouched for this gender discrepancy.

Australian researchers have taken these findings further, because, when it comes to men's emotional health, they do two things exceptionally well. First, they believe that protecting men means exposing the very things that prevent them from emotional well-being, rather than keeping the dysfunctional parts of masculine identity cocooned. And, second, they understand the value of asking men the *right* questions to properly gauge their emotional state. A 2017 longitudinal study among more than 17,000 Australians—conducted by the Household, Income, and Labour Dynamics in Australia (HILDA) and disseminated through Relationships Australia National—found that females are "more likely than males to admit being lonely where the question requires them to label themselves as lonely." But here's the kicker: "Overall levels of loneliness for men are higher than women for all 16 waves of available data."

Perhaps no research delves into this topic with more depth than the 2014 Men's Social Connectedness report. This intensive project analyzed more than 4,100 online surveys from Australian men. This research also included findings from small discussion boards with minority-identifying men, fourteen discussion groups, thirteen ethnographic cases studies, and interviews with mental health practitioners. It culled all of this into a digestible semi-meta-analysis. The report—which focuses on men in their "middle years" between ages thirty-five and fifty-four—found that nearly a quarter of all respondents scored low enough on the industry-standard Duke Social Support Scale to be considered "at risk of social isolation."

This can be attributed to the way men bond—or don't. Half of all respondents said that they rarely talked about deeper personal issues with friends, while 31 percent didn't spend much time talking with their friends in general beyond superficial pleasantries. When respondents were pushed on their preference, nearly a third said they wished they could have more emotionally open, honest conversations with friends, and 28 percent said they wanted friends to open up to them in return. Overall, 37 percent of these men said that they weren't satisfied with the lack of emotional connection and support from their guy friends.

Researchers also employed the Kessler Psychological Distress Scale, or K10, which measures psychological distress, most notably depression and anxiety. They discovered that 17 percent—about one in six—scored very high on the scale for depression and anxiety. Given these honest responses across the board, you might expect many of these men to consider their deficit in social connection a top contender for threats to their health and well-being.

They don't.

According to the authors of the study, these men "rarely feel able to bring their 'neediness' up in conversations, and their loneliness and isolation are rarely, if ever, a topic of public discourse." Perhaps not surprisingly, researchers discovered that these men bore the misery and shame of their situation with a "stoic, masculine pride" rather than try to remedy their lack of social connection. This all-too-common way of handling (or not, as it were) loneliness wouldn't be a problem except for one striking caveat: research now shows a clear connection between social isolation and anxiety, depression, and, in extremes, suicide.

But what about men who enjoy higher degrees of social support? They tested far lower for psychological distress—and, in turn, enjoyed higher rates of mental and emotional resiliency. The workplace is one of the arenas where this has clear economic implications. The 2018

Workplace Loneliness and Job Performance report (conducted among 672 employees and 114 supervisors) found that the greater the sense of loneliness and isolation that an employee feels, the lower his or her job performance and the higher the risk for missed work time.

Common wisdom, not to mention scores of studies, identifies white men fifty and older as the torchbearers of emotional isolation. As many of us know from recent articles on this topic, they are the ones slogging through chronic unemployment; outsourced, phased-out, or undercut careers; higher divorce rates among the upper middle-aged; and a country that increasingly looks far less "white" than the one they've always known. And, truth be told, the politically progressive online media outlets that cater to younger audiences don't exactly help the situation by reflexively invoking the sweeping term "old white men" with utter, uncritical contempt. These are the men whose rate of suicide is spiking.

Yet recent research is showing that older men don't corner the market on social isolation. A national survey conducted by Cigna among 20,000 adults online found that millennials and, especially, Gen Zers scored the highest of any age demographic. This could also be because they are more forthright about their emotional detachment than are older men. The UK Samaritans study mentioned earlier found that men in their twenties, thirties, and forties were the loneliest. Men this age will frequently meet their friends for a beer, but their conversations stay mired at a safe distance in sports, politics, work, and anecdotes that allow them to "flex" or show off to reinforce their masculine status. When they do broach personal struggles, it's far more common for their friends to follow the script, offering solutions but not emotional support. That's a big part of the problem.

———

All of this laconic stoicism might sound good, but it falls woefully short when it comes to men's well-being. Since the 1970s, research has shown that, as one 2018 study among nearly 1,400 adults published in the *Journal of Personality and Social Psychology* revealed, avoiding "negative emotions" is detrimental to one's psychological health. The article, "The Psychological Health Benefits of Accepting Negative Emotions and Thoughts," reported that people who resist negative emotions were more likely to experience symptoms of mood disorders, such as depression, months later, compared with subjects who accepted such emotions. In a blog piece for *Psychology Today*, Otterbein College psychologist Noam Shpancer riffed on that study, specifically the residue that arises from dodging our deeper emotions. Our minds, he wrote, become a "prison, because after a while you begin to feel the need to avoid many situations, people, experiences and places that may bring the negative emotion to mind, stir it, or remind you of it. And the more you avoid, the weaker you feel, the more your coping skills diminish, and the less of life you can experience."

Matthew D. Lieberman, a UCLA psychologist, neuroscientist, and director of the Social Cognitive Neuroscience Lab, took this a quantitative step further. He and his colleagues conducted research in which they showed people pictures of an angry or fearful face, which triggered activity in the amygdala, the part of the brain where our fear-based reactions originate. Yet when participants were asked to use words to describe the angry expression in the photograph, there was a decreased response in the amygdala. Using these words activated a different part of the brain, the ventrolateral prefrontal cortex that is linked to thinking in words about emotions and emotional experiences. Lieberman observed in an article published in the journal *Psychological Science*, "When you put feelings into words, you're activating this prefrontal region and seeing a reduced response in the amygdala. In the same way you hit the brake when you're driving when you see a yellow light, when you put feelings into words, you seem to be hitting the brakes on your emotional responses." Men learning greater fluency about "negative" emotions could mitigate their fear and, in turn, hostility—and it could bring greater joy, as well. "This is ancient wisdom," Lieberman added. "Putting our feelings into words helps us heal better."

It's not difficult to see the connection in all of this. Men who avoid their deeper emotional lives decrease their resiliency. Those who learn to embrace their emotions are more resilient.

Right about now, some readers are surely incredulous, insisting that the Marlboro Man / Clint Eastwood / Marvel action hero characters are the ones who are *really* resilient. They don't whine or wallow in their fear or sadness or any other emotion that only paralyzes or emasculates—they suck it up and get the job done! (Even my enlightened, intelligent, progressive-minded students of all genders struggle not to buy into this mindset.) Yes, they often get the job done—but, as the research above indicates, at a dear cost. Even if men who swallow back their feelings (other than anger) are happy to do so at the expense of their psychological and physiological health, they run the risk of developing a chronic condition that impairs and burdens the intimate relationships in their lives.

Alexithymia is a personality disorder in which people lose the ability to identify and describe their own emotions. People with alexithymia lack social attachment, struggle with relating to others, and have difficulty with empathy (recognizing and understanding the emotions of others). They also have difficulty distinguishing emotional states from bodily sensations. Unlike people born with Asperger's syndrome, who can experience and feel empathy, people with alexithymia do not. This isn't some rare genetic affliction. Sadly, it's fairly common because of how it develops—mostly during early childhood. Psychologists place the percentage of people worldwide navigating alexithymia between 5 and 13 percent. Several researchers have found that it's caused by distress and inconsistent connections between mothers and their infants and in childhood households where the expression of emotion is discouraged. Given that these two factors most commonly occur for male children, this places boys at far greater risk of developing alexithymia. A 2018 study authored by researchers from the University of British Columbia and published in the *Journal of Counseling Psychology*, "Attachment Avoidance, Alexithymia, and Gender," found that alexithymia was associated with attachment avoidance in relationships and a deep-seated fear of emotional disclosure, especially among men. A 2004 study conducted by four Italian psychologists, "Adult Attachment Style and Alexithymia," found that this unsteady attachment style becomes a legacy. The researchers wrote that "the most important finding of this study is that poor parental bonding is related to the perceived difficulty in articulating feeling" later in life, which is "transmitted" to future generations.

After using the industry-standard Toronto Scale of Alexithymia for years while working with male patients, psychologist Ronald Levant noticed something. Levant is a past director of Boston University's Fatherhood Project, on the faculty of Harvard Medical School, and a past president of the American Psychological Association. When he notices something, it's worth paying attention. Time after time, in both his practice and his research, he noticed patterns. "Nobody polices gender identity like boys do," Levant told me, pointing out how boys choose games that promote competition, toughness, and stoicism.

The boys and men Levant worked with weren't necessarily textbook cases of alexithymia, but every one of them exhibited similar symptoms—most notably an inability to access and put into words feelings that, coincidentally, were considered off-limits for most males: joy, sadness, fear, shame, guilt. This drastically impacted every part of their lives, especially friendships and romantic relationships. Levant told me they had a "subclinical version" of alexithymia. This condition was rooted in a worldview and largely predictable behaviors that many males followed blindly. This "subclinical" version is all too common.

When we spoke, Levant echoed research that has found that, while huge swaths of men follow this script to varying degrees, rigid adherence is more densely concentrated among less educated men. "Data supports this," he said. "The lower the education, the lower the income, the stronger men endorse traditional masculine norms." From these close observations, he coined the term "normative male alexithymia (NMA)." Eventually, he and colleague Glenn Good developed a diagnostic barometer, the Normative Male Alexithymia Scale, which was the first to "measure and show the direct link between traditional masculine socialization" and its emotionally numbing fallout, according to Levant.

Levant also developed a therapeutic manual for men faced with NMA. In his sessions with patients, he gave men a vocabulary for naming the emotions they could recognize in others but not in themselves. When patients complained about feeling "hassled" or "burned out," he had them drill down to the word "stressed" instead. For some feelings, however, there were no replacements. "These guys had no words to describe happiness, joy, fear, sadness, grief. It was much easier to get these men to identify emotions in other people than in themselves." To help remedy this, he had them observe other people and keep a log about what they observed. He also had them describe their own bodily sensations (say, a tightness in their chest or a clenching in their guts) and pushed them to connect these sensations with words or actions that affected them directly or indirectly. Then he had them look on a vocabulary list and assign their physical sensations a "feeling." Techniques such as these are now commonly used by practitioners who work with emotionally repressed men. Levant focused on teaching his patients how to make these connections because, as he told me, "When it comes to human relationships, without language you've got no tools to work with."

This was John's struggle. (John was the IT executive mentioned in the Introduction.) When I first spoke with him three years ago, the father of two young daughters was fighting to save his marriage of more than twenty years. From his own admission, John was so disconnected from his emotions that he couldn't understand why his wife wouldn't appreciate the logic and rationale of the facts he routinely leaned on when something he said or did hurt her feelings. "Time after time after time," he told me, "I ended up defending myself by telling her the facts of what happened. And she often came back by asking, 'Where in there are my feelings?'" It wasn't that John didn't want to push beyond the cold, hard security of facts, because he did. But something old and deep always prevented him. "Even though my mind was telling me what she wanted when she shared her pain or frustration, I was afraid that she would see me as weak if I admitted that maybe I was wrong, or if I apologized." Despite the intellectual awareness of what his wife was asking for—and of wanting to meet that need—John just didn't know how to open himself up in such a nakedly vulnerable way. "I don't remember my parents ever talking about emotions. Everything was about facts. I never doubted my father's love, but it wasn't ever discussed. It was under the covers—to me and to my mother."

Once he experienced the mounting pressures of career, marriage, family life, and pursuing success, John became even more isolated. "It got to the point where I could no longer tell anyone what I enjoyed in life," he confessed.

When I first spoke with John, at the outset of my research, I was convinced that his experience was an anomaly. Surely, this wasn't the case with many well-educated men, because research shows that they aren't nearly as beholden to traditional masculine values as less-educated men. I was wrong.

When his marriage began to dissolve, Harris doubled down on an impulse he had always relied on: being the fixer. "My job was to fix things, to make other people happy," the Ivy League college administrator told me. His sense of empathy and compassion for others had always been strong, he said, but he lost a sense of self-identity. He gradually lost touch with the few close friends he had because, by his own admission, he was so "fixated" on trying to salvage a contentious, doomed marriage, trying to be there for his children, and maintaining a demanding career. The more disconnected he became from without, the more this occurred from within. Men's self-identity originates from the external messages they receive from other men, and, in turn, they internalize them. "The way we socialize boys is through disconnection, which starts with the self," Terry Real, a psychologist, author, and expert on men and their relationships, told me. He identifies patriarchy as the cause of this. Virtually every man he has worked with in his private practice, he said, "is struggling with forms of disconnection."

This was the root of Harris's problem. "I lacked self-intimacy," he told me. "I got to a point where I no longer had any idea who I was. It never crossed my mind to ask myself, What do I want?" At work he was decisive and capable. Outside of work, however, he would question his own competence. "I couldn't even order dinner for myself when I started dating again. I'd tell waiters, 'I'll have what she's having.'"

Paul summed up this problem best when he told me, "This is what's hobbling us as guys. We don't have what we need to make the most important connection—with ourselves."

———

When we talk about this profound linguistic disconnect in many males, we're actually talking about more than their inability to articulate. We're talking about a central, defining fear that girds and informs every word in the script: vulnerability. As the previous chapter about vulnerability discussed, this form of emotional exposure hasn't been viewed over the past hundred years in our culture with any nuance. Men who exhibit it—unless they do so within the small window of arbitrary acceptance or they enjoy great status or power—are considered failures as men. This is why so many men refuse to ask for help of any kind, lest they appear vulnerable. This axiom holds true in all areas of men's lives, because nothing—absolutely nothing—is considered more verboten than the appearance of vulnerability.

As we've learned over the past few years, many men fifty and older would rather fade into depression, isolation, and even suicide—yes, the very things they dread—than seek help finding or maintaining friendships. If all of this weren't bad enough, this self-sabotaging reflex is compounded by a thoroughly American ethos that asking for help and giving in to solitude and introspection is nothing short of a moral failure. Psychologist Glenn Good, who researches masculinity and whose private practice focuses on men's issues, maintains that none of this has anything to do with the Y chromosome. It's all upbringing. "Men *learn* to seek less help," he has written.

Most men create and maintain friendships through a dynamic psychologists describe as "side by side" or "shoulder to shoulder." That is, most men bond through shared activities like watching televised sports over beers, mountain biking, working out together, or playing poker. Conversely, many women connect face-to-face through conversations, which foster greater emotional honesty. (There are exceptions in gender identities, obviously.) As the previous chapter revealed, millennials and Gen Zers are the first generations of young men actively pushing back to some degree against these restrictive norms in their friendships. Geoffrey Greif, a sociologist with the University of Maryland School of Social Work, has played in a biweekly poker game for more than fifty years with a lot of the same men. He shared with me that this isn't a "place where feelings are being brought up." That said, one of the players took a chance and shared that he had bladder cancer and had recently had his prostate removed. Even though some of the guys didn't know about this, "it held up the game for only five minutes," Greif said, "not forty-five minutes." Given the limited response and his sick friend's vulnerability, Greif said he thought about "suggesting a group hug, but it didn't seem appropriate."

This is what often happens when men connect "shoulder to shoulder." The expectation is that the activity and lack of emotional disclosure will predominate because many men rely on such time for avoidance—from problems or stressors with family or work and even from themselves. When kept in balance, this can be healthy, but for many men this is the rule, rather than the exception. The problems with this dynamic are that it perpetuates men's emotional repression and atrophies the neural synapses they need socially that help them process and understand their deeper feelings. This doesn't mean men need to have therapy sessions when they're out together, watching football games and eating chicken wings. But it allows for more wiggle room against the otherwise implicit expectation that "deep dives" are off-limits. Men do, after all, have problems that need tending. But busy jobs, romantic relationships, and families preclude additional time to discuss these outside of their homes.

None of this is to say that side-by-side friendships don't serve a purpose. Clearly, they do. But men should never maintain friendships exclusively this way because shoulder-to-shoulder bonding makes it even harder for them to develop the "muscles" they sorely need to avoid emotional isolation. Too many men lack awareness of, and the words for, deeper feelings that reveal their vulnerability. "The language of connection is the critical piece for men in their relationships," says psychiatrist Robert Garfield, who cofounded a hub for male-centered therapy near Philadelphia called the Friendship Lab. "The way they speak is a huge reduction in terms of what they communicate and what they don't."

This occurs with devastating dividends, Jacqueline Olds told me. The Harvard psychiatrist, who co-wrote the book *The Lonely American: Drifting Apart in the Twenty-First Century* with her husband, says that not discussing "things that matter makes people feel lonelier, and this is especially true in men." Critics—and there are legions, including many men in the psychological community—maintain that men don't need to learn to communicate with friends face-to-face because many heterosexual men rely on wives or female partners as their confidants. But what happens to these men when they lose these confidants to death, divorce, or breakup? Research shows they become withdrawn or they rush to find another wife, girlfriend, or female friend. Unlike the women in their lives, they haven't been taught the emotional resiliency required to withstand the eroding social landscape.

Many middle-aged men I spoke with, in their fifties to early seventies, insisted that they do seek out a friend, one-on-one, if they need to talk. There's no question that this is a healthy tactic and supports neural connectivity with their deeper emotional lives. But something often gets in the way. When his marriage was unraveling, Harris, the university administrator, resisted reaching out to friends. "It became harder and harder to talk about that stuff. I was a little ashamed that I couldn't fix this. And I was in denial about what was going on." Eventually, one of his friends pushed back and demanded to know what was happening. "I eventually unloaded with him," said Harris. "But not everything."

Paul had a similar experience when a romantic relationship ended after three and a half years. He went out to lunch with a good friend to discuss the distress he was feeling and, in his words, "didn't hold anything back." But, in the same breath, Paul admitted to me,

"At some point, though, I put the brakes on. I don't like to burden people." What's interesting is that both Paul and Harris, articulate and intelligent men, claimed at first to open up and talk honestly with a friend when they sorely needed a confidant. Yet in the next breath, they admitted that they "put the brakes on."

Similarly, Jay told me that he will open up in his men's support group, which is facilitated by a psychiatrist. But the entrepreneur-turned-philanthropist doesn't extend what he's learned about sharing beyond the group's bubble. "It's not safe in the real world. If I share my feelings, they might be open to misinterpretation when there aren't the same ground rules."

This was something I heard over and over when I sat in on men's groups. Members of these groups gushed about how they had never experienced, anywhere else, the kind of support, permission, and safety in which to talk openly and, most urgently, to learn how to access and process their deeper feelings, as they did in these circles. Yet they didn't feel safe—and that's really the issue here—using these new skills beyond the closed door of the group. The thirty-something therapist from Frederick, Maryland, who runs the men's group I observed, told me that his friendships from the past are still "locked in the old dynamic where there's no emotional honesty or vulnerability." And he would like more of this. Why won't he apply what he's learned and teaches to his clients with his own friends? "I'm too scared to try to change [those relationships]," he confessed.

Of course, men have every right to determine the extent of disclosure about their lives with whomever they choose. And it's true that many men don't like to "burden" others with their problems. This is why they don't ask questions about psychic or emotional pain they observe in another guy. Many men I spoke with admitted they were wary of intruding when they observed pain in another man. "The plain truth of it is that intimacy is just too hot to handle for many men," Garfield told me. "At work men never avoid asking questions and never handle topics so superficially—they ask for the details of a problem." But they shy away from asking the important questions. Once you encourage men to start doing this, though, they can. "They all show they have the capacity to ask probing questions of each other," Garfield said. "Here's an example of what I'm talking about—they do it with women but choose not to with men."

Another reason so many men experience their emotional disclosure in fits and starts has to do with control. The need to appear in control, capable, and successful forces males to scrutinize everything they say in front of other guys so that they don't slip and betray the "wrong" kind of vulnerability. This is why so many men lean into the facts of an experience. Paul had no problem telling his close friend the facts of how the relationship with his girlfriend had unraveled, but he stopped short of divulging the deeper emotional strife he was experiencing. John, who struggled with feeling his own emotions, would tell his ex-wife "the facts of what happened" when arguments arose between them.

Facts are safe. They're logical. They seem to be conveniently indisputable. They also sidestep emotions and feelings. In other words, they cover any missteps of vulnerability. This is also why many men seek out male friends when they want advice and clear-cut answers to problems. They seek pragmatism and solutions. Now, everyone could benefit from this brand of well-intentioned, thoughtful, logical counseling at times, but it doesn't provide emotional support. And it doesn't prevent loneliness.

One of the least-discussed, least-understood factors that contributes to loneliness for straight men in their romantic relationships comes from an unlikely corner: their partners. In her book *Daring*

Greatly, vulnerability researcher and author Brené Brown reveals that many women are "constantly criticizing [men] for not being open and vulnerable and intimate. . . . Here's the painful pattern that emerged from my research with men: We ask them to be vulnerable, we beg them to let us in, and we plead with them to tell us when they're afraid, but the truth is that most women can't stomach it. In those moments when real vulnerability happens in men, most of us recoil with fear and that fear manifests as everything from disappointment to disgust."

————

One of the least discussed factors contributing to men's inability to connect more openly has everything to do with the way they're taught to negotiate the world. The book *The Psychology of Friendship*, edited by Mahzad Hojjat, observes that "both gender-role socialization theory and empirical findings suggest that boys are "trained" from an early age to be competitive." It's taught to boys so young that it becomes part of their subconscious and infiltrates their male friendships. We're not talking garden-variety competition here, though. The authors of the chapter on competition and friendship in this book noted: "The norms for male-male friendships seem to discourage communal expression or sentimentality at all cost while encouraging direct competition and 'one-upmanship.'" Dominating other males with a *Lord of the Flies* ferocity—which even takes the subtle form of one guy making his buddy look "bad" in front of others to increase his perceived status—is far more admired than it is discouraged, and it isn't quelled until boys or young men unwittingly take it too far. This is why many males see the world as a dark, brutish place.

This lens colors so much about men's worldview that it will inevitably taint their friendships with other guys in the form of competition.

Ian shared with me the difficulty of learning to open up in his men's group, which is facilitated by a mental health professional, with other men who are equally successful in terms of wealth and career status. "You're in a room together, sitting in a circle, there's serious eye contact, and it's incumbent on you not to bullshit the group. Which is hard, because everyone's waiting for someone else to make the first move and risk vulnerability." The architect said that, even though he's been part of this group for nearly a decade, old habits die hard. Very hard. He still fights the impulse to compare himself—with guys in the group, with business associates, with friends. He still feels threatened when one of these guys buys a new car he covets, when he hears about their shrewd investments, or when they appear to be in better physical shape than him. "We spend a lot of time talking about vulnerability, especially in our family and romantic relationships. It takes you a while to learn that this isn't a bad thing." It took a long time, but once he and his group members learned to trust that they could share openly, honestly, in front of other men—once they pushed beyond the need to "strut our stuff in front of each other," as he said—the degree of disclosure took off. "It's incredibly liberating," he said, "to sit there, vulnerable, with no pretext. Nothing works better than this for getting rid of the layers of crud you've heaped up from years of being a guy."

Most men either aren't aware of how pervasive this sense of competition is or of the extent to which it erodes their trust. But Dwayne, the publisher and editor of a men's magazine, is. It's the reason he turned his back on male friendships throughout his adult life. "I always struggled with constant competition in friendships," he told me. "Even with my brother. The constant drag of everything being about who's better at this, who's got the best car, who's got the hottest girlfriend. Guys spend their whole time together ripping each other. When I was younger, I always felt like I was being judged by other guys. Like I wasn't measuring up as a man, because I couldn't repair my car." So, when the relationship with Dwayne's first wife grew rocky, he sated his need for deeper connection by reaching out to other women—who could meet him where he was without the baggage of distrust (born from competition) getting in the way.

One of the things that surprised me when I interviewed boys and men was how fierce they were in their loyalty to friends. Whether they were fifteen or fifty years old, many of them spoke in stereo, with unflinching fealty, about the golden retriever–like devotion they felt for their closest friends. Loyalty tops the list of qualities many men (and boys) appreciate in their close male friendships. Males of all ages spoke with passion about the "trust" they have in their close friends, because they knew that these guys could keep secrets. This is why, says Harvard psychiatrist Jacqueline Olds, so many men get so angry with their wives or female partners. They feel "betrayed" if these partners share details about their relationships with friends or family members.

And yet, one of the great ironies of male friendships is how quickly men cut bait, so to speak, with friends if some obstacle prevents them from getting together regularly, face-to-face. Psychologists call this common disconnect—this tacit acceptance that male intimacy is subject to an "out of sight, out of mind" mindset—the Male Deficit Model. This occurs when a male friend moves out of town, stops taking part in a shared activity, or becomes a father. The Men and Social Connectedness report found that "a majority (61 percent) have lost contact with more friends than they would like in the past few years." This happens to a lesser degree for men as they age—due to struggles with injury, illness, mental health, unemployment, and finances—but it hits younger men hardest. "The most vulnerable time for friendships is during our ascendancy stage," according to Robert Garfield.

During the ascendancy stage, men typically first experience big life changes—marriage, children, and a greater focus on career. "This is when friends drop to the rock bottom of the list," Garfield told me. Unlike women in this stage, who look to extend their network for greater resources, men retreat in the opposite direction. They double down on their perceived roles as primary providers and protectors, leaning further into the belief that they're failing if they don't take on these responsibilities alone. "This becomes a model for adult life with many younger men," Garfield said. "[They put] away what they perceive as the 'childhood needs' of friendship: sharing emotional intimacies and supporting each other."

Given all of these variables, it's no surprise that men don't support each other on a large scale. Sure, men do take to social media, and from the late nineteenth century through the late twentieth century fraternal organizations (think: Knights of Columbus, Rotarians, Elks, even the Masons) offered men webs of social support. But most of these outlets have largely been utilized for business networking—for getting a leg up on the competition. Men don't work at creating social networks for the purpose of emotional support. They never have. Women do, of course. A 2017 Danish study published in the online journal *PLOS ONE* conducted among 800 college freshmen focused on the role of gender in building social networks, especially when it came to "mobility behavior" on smartphones. In "The Role of Gender in Social Network Organization," the four researchers observed that women sent text messages and communicated through social media more often with other females, and—this is crucial—that they also shared more personal information than did male participants. This squared with previous research that found that young women tend to form gender-insular social groups with one another throughout childhood and again as adults. Conversely, according to the study's authors, men "are shown to increase their female contacts as they get older," as a means of emotional support. This networking continues in their romantic relationships: "Women are taught to be keepers of psychological health in their relationships," says Jaqueline Olds. This includes building and maintaining relationships that benefit both of them and the rest of the family. Men might be aware of this impulse to keep relationships healthy, but, Olds told me, they "don't say anything, because it might feel effeminate or infantile to them. It's not in keeping with the manly ideal in America."

Many men I interviewed confessed to happily letting their wives orchestrate their shared social lives, a template they picked up from their own parents. This reflexive passivity plays out beyond the home, as well—even in public bathrooms. Research shows that women are more sociable and relaxed in public bathrooms; they are far more likely to help each other, for instance, sharing toilet paper between stalls and even supportive words if another woman seems upset. Men, however, perceive public bathrooms like a dark city street—an embattled space where utter silence prevails and eyes are kept riveted straight ahead but never on another guy. The fear revolves around homophobia in a space where men believe themselves to be vulnerable because their pants are down, literally and figuratively.

My son first learned about this protocol (not the reasons for it) when he was five. While we were in a men's bathroom at Valley Forge National Park, a site that interprets an important stage of the American Revolution, he approached a guy in his late forties or early fifties who was peeing at a urinal. "Are you with the British army?" my son asked, referencing the Union Jack on the back of the man's fleece jacket. When the man didn't answer, my son asked again, louder. The man finished, zipped up, and turned around, his face flush. He still didn't answer. Another man was exiting a stall, and the guy in the fleece said to him, "Looks like this little guy hasn't gotten the memo yet about talking in the john."

What does this have to do with men's failure to create social networks? A lot, actually. So much about the ways men choose to interface with other males in public spaces speaks to their unwillingness to extend themselves to each other; this erodes social capital. I have struggled with this lack of a social web myself. When my son, now eight, was a toddler, I took him to music classes and library story times and sing-alongs that were populated, to a large extent, by young mothers and their daughters. Still, I didn't feel like an outlier because I have had many female friends throughout my life. In fact, I was looking forward to trading notes with some of them about first-time parenthood and maybe even receiving some reassuring words and advice. Yet I quickly discovered that the moms would recoil if I tried to initiate conversation.

When I asked a small group of moms if my son could join a circle of girls playing musical instruments, one mother summed up a sentiment I experienced quite a bit: "I'm sorry, but this circle is really just for the girls. I'm sure you can understand." The other mothers nodded. This sentiment seems to be a growing one and played out in a letter a young mother wrote to *Washington Post* advice columnist Carolyn Hax. The mother complained about a father who asked if his toddler son could join a group of young girls on a public playground. Hax called out the female writer for practicing the same gender-based exclusionary tactic that she had accused men of using.

The oppression women have experienced forever has taught them the importance of extended support webs. I observed this on Meetup.com. In the nearest city to where I live there were eighteen groups for men to bond through such activities as cycling, basketball, fishing, motorcycle clubs, and barbershop quartets. Outside of an evangelical group or a support group for gay men or men of color, no others existed. When it came to support groups geared exclusively toward women, I stopped counting at 200. While these groups also offered bonding through activities (motorcycle club, drinking wine, girls' night out, book club), there was a far greater depth and breadth of groups aimed at meeting the deeper needs of its members—divorce support, seekers of wisdom, life coaching, fitness, self-esteem, menopause support, millennial girl power, wives in challenging marriages. A Reddit user from Denver had a similar observation: he found that a search in his area for Meetup.com groups for men netted 103 results, which were largely activity based (the few support groups listed were run by the same female therapist). Activity and support groups for women totaled 449.

Perhaps no other research puts this social network deficit in context—and defines the tragic outcomes more starkly—as does a 2018 study published in the *American Journal of Men's Health*. Three public health researchers from New Zealand with a specialty in suicide prevention observed how men place far more importance on smaller networks for emotional support than do women and too often limit their disclosure about the issues and problems that most trouble them. This study, "Masculinity, Social Connectedness, and Mental Health: Men's Diverse Patterns of Practice," explores the "weight of social taboos in [men's] social connections with other men," which encourages them to follow risky old patterns: they either secretly confide in female friends so they don't publicly jeopardize their masculine image, or swallow back their deeper feelings and risk "significant impacts on men's mental health." The New Zealand researchers cited additional studies which found that "young distressed men" who wanted "closer social connections and support from family members and friends . . . feared being judged as emotionally vulnerable, weak, and unmasculine." Their silence left them at "heightened risk of suicide." Men value social relationships that "provide instrumental support" where they can do activities together but where deeper connection and support are lacking, unlike women whose friendships often proffer emotional support. When middle-aged men were depressed and experienced loneliness and sadness, some of them wanted to share these feelings with loved ones but, according to the study, didn't "know how to talk about these feelings or felt embarrassed to do so." (Researchers cited many studies that pointed to the ubiquitous pattern in which men save their deeper emotional concerns and struggles for their intimate female partners.) Just as tragic, these men had "few or no people in their social networks" they trusted enough to "share their feelings" with.

Part of what holds men back, observe the study authors, are the negative experiences in disclosing personal issues with other men who have been unwilling or unreceptive to discussing them. Another factor, which I've observed myself and have heard from boys and men I interviewed, is that the competition that informs so many male relationships breeds a deep distrust, which prevents them from feeling safe opening up to male friends. Why risk sharing something that makes you feel vulnerable if it might be dismissed, laughed at, or used against you in front of other guys? The researchers cited a study that found that young men who were distressed "desperately wanted closer social connections and support from family members and friends," but "they feared being judged as emotionally vulnerable, weak, and un-masculine." Ultimately, this lack of social and emotional networks has "negative implications for men's social connectedness and mental well-being," the researchers observed, putting younger men, especially, at "heightened risk of suicide."

A lot of the conversation about men and their loneliness has centered exclusively around the need for men to have more friendships. There's no doubt that this helps mitigate some of their isolation. But here's the thing: if they're not being taught to bond in ways that help them get beyond their old safe pattern of doing activities together without talking about and better understanding the deeper issues that define their lives—and the feelings connected with them—then a considerable degree of their loneliness will continue. What's more, who will they turn to when older friendships or romantic relationships fizzle out or end in death? This is where an expanded social network can have a profound impact on men's lives, often more so than one or two close male friendships.

Bill knows about this striking difference in support systems. The fifty-year-old Frederick, Maryland, resident did what a lot of loving, well-intentioned men do—he devoted much of his time and energy to his marriage and his children at the expense of male friendships. "I thought that that was what I was supposed to do to be a good family man," he told me. Once his marriage was in trouble, Bill, an artisan who makes currency printing plates for the federal government, was faced with some hard truths he had pushed down for a long time. "I couldn't understand why my family life was not turning out the way I thought it would," he told me. "My kids didn't appreciate the sacrifices I made for them, and my wife was having affairs." This was when he realized "I'd had low-grade depression for twenty years. That's how long I had been miserable, trying to make everyone happy."

He didn't seek professional help, but he did turn to "life coaches" on YouTube. The YouTube coaches helped him "get my head in a much better place." At their suggestion, he began to "devour" books about human and relationship psychology, he said. He began to feel more inspired and positive about his life, and some of the depression dissipated. Then, last summer, divorce became imminent.

"I was contemplating suicide," he said.

Once again, he turned to his online gurus and followed the suggestion to find a support group. He found some meetup groups that helped, he said, and eventually the veil of depression started to lift, but only temporarily. He realized that he still needed something else: emotional support. He did have a few male friends—including one from high school with whom he could discuss "life issues" while jogging. But deeper disclosure was still missing. He had made male friends throughout adulthood, but "I didn't feel like I could talk to them," he said. "You feel like you're inconveniencing them. Besides, it was pretty clear that most of them didn't care enough to want to know" about his private life. On advice from his estranged wife's therapist, he found a male therapist (the same one who felt uneasy seeking out a male therapist for his own needs) who, after working with Bill for a month or so, suggested he join the men's group he co-facilitated.

Along with therapy, this group helped Bill burn away the fog of depression for longer stretches of time. "When I started doing the men's group, I found something I never had with my male friends. Because we're all strangers to each other and don't have the same social circle on the outside, it's nice that you know that what you say in there won't come back to you. This makes it a lot easier to open up." Bill also discovered another perk that eats away at his depression. "For so long I thought that the low self-image I had was only me," he told me one evening when I observed his men's group. "I thought most guys didn't struggle with this. But I've learned that these other guys feel this way, too. There's other people going through this, too. I'm not so alone after all."

When I caught up with John again two years after our initial conversation, the change in him was remarkable. Rarely have I witnessed such a radical shift in an adult in such a small window of time. Since we last spoke, he had persuaded his wife to go into couples therapy. During their separation (and eventual divorce), John started practicing mindfulness and meditation, which helped him better access his deeper feelings. This opened his eyes to something that seemed oddly familiar. One woman he dated spent a week in the hospital, and John often called her to check in. "I'd ask her how she was feeling, and she'd tell me about her test results. She wouldn't talk about how she was feeling. She couldn't understand the difference between what was happening to her and how it impacted her emotionally." The irony wasn't lost on him. "This had been me."

Ever since John learned how to open the pipeline to his deeper feelings and to create a richer inner life, he's become more aware of the limitations of his male friendships. This was summed up in the relationship he had with a friend he lived with for nine months after separating from his wife. "He's a very nice, caring guy," John said. "But when I tried to have conversations with more emotional teeth, he talked about nothing but golf and retirement. So I spent a lot of time having those conversations with his girlfriend." Now that he's more aware of this disconnect in so many men, John has grown fatalistic. "It's frustrating, disappointing, and sad to know that I'm probably never going to get [deeper connections] from these friends."

If men like John keep looking for greater intimacy with others who just don't have the will to reciprocate—men who want to keep the pipelines to their deeper feelings shut—they will keep coming up with the same unfulfilling result. But Robert Garfield says that this lonely realization isn't cause for despair. "When you commit to being your deeper, truer self, you're leaving the isolation of no-man's-land behind and entering the world of connection and relationships. It's scary and lonely at times, especially early on, but it gives you access to a friend you didn't know was there before. That's you. You discover a dialogue that wasn't there before. This allows you to have a far better relationship with yourself and, eventually, with other people."

This very thing happened to Ian. Since he learned to let down his guard in his support group, he now identifies with this complex shift. He said that he feels more "alone," which proved to be a good thing. His constant compulsion to compete with other guys beefed up his need to set himself apart from them. Now that he views himself as "less unique," as he described it, he feels more connected to the guys in his group. "I often felt I was going through something no one else was or that they could understand," he said. "Knowing that your heart has the same valves as the guy next to you helps you become more trusting of other people."

In May 2014, Paul had one of those experiences we read about. He had gone into the hospital after feeling chest pain, a rapid heartbeat, shortness of breath, and lightheadedness. Doctors discovered four life-threatening pulmonary embolisms. "They told me I could drop dead at any moment," he said. "That was when I decided that for the rest of my life I wanted to be happy. Beforehand, I thought I was a laid-back guy, but, really, I was so black and white about so much in my life, even after everything with my ex-wife. This helped me soften the edges a lot."

For Paul, greater happiness and softer edges meant he had to push past his deeper fears and a lifetime of suppressed sensitivity, both of which had gnawed at his deeper connection to himself and, in turn, others. The answer: "I needed to lean into the thing I resisted."

For the first time in his adult life, that didn't mean looking for another romantic relationship. If that came along, well, great, but "I realized that I needed friends."

This quest for new friends has happened at a "glacial pace," but "I so much enjoy the contact now more than I used to. I have some friends at work, and I have some running buddies." Someone he used to work with reached out to Paul, and they started meeting for lunch every six weeks or so. The deeper, let alone frequent, connections aren't there to the extent that Paul would like, but something unexpected occurred. The way he viewed connection radically shifted. "I just try to be open when I'm out at the grocery store or at work. It's been very healthy for me—even just talking about anything with an office mate or waiting in line at the store."

There's a bleaker side to this journey, though, one that isn't pleasant or easy to hear someone admit without feeling some degree of sorrow. But it underscores the great courage, honesty, grit, and self-actualization someone like Paul has shown in his pursuit of connection. "Sometimes I go out to dinner by myself literally to have someone to talk to when I order food. Or just to be around other people."

Still, it's worth it, says Paul. "I've got to be honest with myself if I'm going to move forward. I can't ignore or push my feelings down anymore. This helps me do that."

A year later I emailed Paul to see where things were on his sojourn. In addition to joining a weekly trivia team (no deep connections, though), he was also "considering starting a meetup group for lonely, middle-aged men."

The truth is that many men desire what Paul is pursuing with dogged, fearless intent. Yet they can't bring themselves to go after it. This was what Robert Garfield and five colleagues discovered through the Men's Friendship and Emotional Intimacy Survey, which gauged the degree of emotional intimacy men felt with their closest male friends and whether they valued emotional intimacy in these friendships. After gleaning completed surveys from 381 men between the ages of eighteen and eighty-seven (the mean age was thirty-six), Garfield and his colleagues reported that most of the respondents had at least two close friends, while a quarter of them enjoyed close friendships with one or two men. The survey asked them to gauge the depth and breadth of their intimacy based on their willingness to disclose intimate details about themselves. It surveyed their willingness to openly express deeper feelings with these friends, especially the extent to which they made themselves vulnerable enough to share their perceived "weaknesses," as the survey termed it. They were also asked if they ever provided the same brand of deeper emotional support back to their friends (both through words and physical affection). And the survey mined the extent to which the participants worked together with their friends toward common goals. (Interestingly, the researchers equated "vulnerability" and "weaknesses.") Forty-three percent of the respondents said that they experienced a "medium level" of these qualities in their friendships, while a quarter experienced and contributed few of these qualities. For all of the progress many younger men, especially, have been making with showing greater physical affection with their male friends, nearly half of the respondents admitted that "other people's judgment" in public did limit their willingness to give a hug, touch a friend during conversation, or even stand or sit in close proximity.

Still, more than 60 percent of all survey respondents wished they had "greater emotional closeness" with their male friends, Garfield wrote in his book, *Breaking the Male Code: Unlocking the Power of Friendship*. Why? Perhaps these men know, deep down, what's gained by males who give and receive this form of intimacy in their friendships. Garfield observed that the "more emotional closeness men had with their male friends, the more they desired to both increase their number of male friends and deepen the emotional intimacy with male friends they currently have." Time after time, "males with greater intimacy in their male friendships had higher levels of support," regardless of their age, race, ethnicity, and socioeconomic status. This translated into support in the "most intimate and important areas of men's lives—relationships, parenting, sex, health, and work," said Garfield. These findings were echoed, by the way, in the Australian Men and Social Connectedness report, which revealed that many men want greater openness with their friends and to be able to talk about personal problems. That said, respondents confessed they don't typically have the skills or tools to initiate these conversations; nor do they understand how to respond when a friend opens up to them. For all of the press about the depth and breadth of intimacy between male friends in their twenties and thirties, the survey revealed that the intimacy many of them desire still eludes them.

While it's true that many younger men are "bonded with their guy friends," Garfield observed, "they're not necessarily sharing the most vulnerable feelings and questions" with each other. This can result in unhealthy behaviors down the road. When they were asked what they wished they had more of in their friendships, 33 percent said they wanted to both give and receive more support from their closest male friends, while nearly one-fifth said they wanted a "greater level of vulnerability."

————

Eventually, Dwayne (the guy who had developed a deep distrust of other males because of the toxic competition that arises between them) remarried. In 2011, he and his wife had stillborn twin daughters. He tried to "stuff it down" by drinking and an old impulse: finding succor through deep, platonic connection with other women. As with so many men, he lost touch with his deeper emotions because he was "afraid that if I expressed certain things I'd be rejected and perceived as less manly" by others, including his wife. The irony in all of this was that, for all of his resentment of the men throughout his life who had ridiculed him if he openly expressed sensitivity, he had followed their lead by suppressing these feelings.

Therapy brought his marriage back from the precipice and opened his eyes to two inescapable truths: he needed to find friendships in which he could vent his grief and sadness, and it had to be with other men.

This was no small, easy step for a man who grew to resent men throughout his adult life. What changed all of that was the birth of his son when Dwayne was forty-three. The birth became the impetus for starting a men's magazine where, for the first time in his life, he was able to attract men to him "who are honest with themselves and able to openly talk about their failings and to accept them." More pressing, he felt a new "urgency for [my son's] sake. I needed to learn how to become vulnerable again with men, so my son could eventually learn, too. I needed to relearn how to be in meaningful friendships with men that didn't involve competition." There was another reason he knew he needed to do this. "Three years ago, I was in danger of becoming that guy—who withdraws more and more into himself with time," said Dwayne, who suffers from chronic depression.

In the summer of 2015, he attempted to form a dads' group, asking the fathers of his son's friends if they would join. A group of twelve to twenty-four men still meet monthly at a local craft brewery. He does get frustrated with the tenor of the conversation at times. "I'm often thinking, *You're drinking beer and watching sports on the TV. Do we really have to talk about it, too?*" Still, it's helping him better understand the kinds of men he has spent a lifetime avoiding. "I'm relearning my responses to guys. Before, if there were a lot of guys getting really aggressive and competitive, I would get annoyed and turned inward or leave. Now I'm conscious of how I can be more empathetic to the reasons why some guys might be doing it." To his surprise, his marriage has benefited, as well. Developing this new kind of intimacy with men has helped him "practice being more vulnerable with my wife," helping this relationship grow "stronger and deeper." Collaterally, it has taught him to "let go of the feeling that I have to demonstrate some superhuman strength" in front of her.

What Dwayne is doing and accomplishing is nothing short of astounding, let alone unheard of in most male circles outside of structured men's groups. Despite a lifetime of deep, painful scars and distrust from the many ways other males, including friends and his own brother, devalued his identity as a man—and for the way he devalued himself, in turn—he is learning to forgive and accept other men. Perhaps most difficult, he is learning to meet them where they are emotionally and not to demand they do the same for him. It's paying off.

For the first time in a long time, he says, he has a "group of guys I consider friends. We hang out other times, too. Sometimes I'll get a text from a guy in the group, asking to meet for a beer, and I'll know that he needs to talk about something important. There are guys I will talk to about the challenges of marriage, the experience that I went through with [his stillborn daughters], and the struggles of being a father." He pushes through and keeps the group going, always with the needs of his son—and other boys—not far from his mind. He talked about observing his young son interacting with his male friends, holding hands, their heads against each other, and talking so intently. "Their love and affection for each other is so precious. I don't want them to lose that." So he models this behavior among these boys with his own male friends. "I've started hugging friends when I greet them." And he hugs his good friends' sons. "I want them to experience good and healthy affection from other men."

Dwayne stops short of calling his progress anywhere near complete. "I don't know that it's completely happened (finding deeper connection with guys in the group). On my end, my willingness to share and be vulnerable with other guys hasn't fully developed, and I still have a difficult time asking for help." Still, he has witnessed a deep shift within himself. "It's been healing being in this group."

CHAPTER SEVEN

Men and Violence—
Shame and the Damage Done

One early June night six years ago, two months before my son's second birthday, I was driving to Maine when I pulled off of I-84 to get dinner. A few miles earlier, I had passed a sign for the Blue Colony Diner in southwestern Connecticut and decided to head there because I was hungry, and I wanted to wait out a summer downpour. As I pulled open the diner's glass door, I saw something that literally knocked the wind out of me. It was a sticker the size of a grapefruit with a cartoon image of a teddy bear with wings, cradling a much smaller teddy bear. Above the bears were the words "Always Here, Never Forgotten," and beneath them, completing the circle, "26 Angels."

I was in Newtown.

Much of the hour or so I spent in the diner was a blur. It was one of the few times in my life when I had gone somewhere public, a diner no less, and felt like I was intruding simply by being there. I kept my eyes on my plate as I ate, partly because I felt like an interloper and partly because I felt dizzy. When I paid my bill at the cash register, I saw twenty-six paper cutouts on a window behind the register—the same teddy bears with the names of the young children and their teachers killed at nearby Sandy Hook Elementary School. When I walked outside, the rain had stopped, and the sun was peeking through a dusk sky that was clearing into brilliant hues of peach and orange.

I wasn't sure why I did what I did next. Perhaps I felt a compulsion to unobtrusively pay my respects, or maybe it was a gnawing need to force myself to consider, even if just momentarily and from a remove, what these school and mass shooting epidemics must mean for parents everywhere. I found Sandy Hook Village once I passed over a small bridge and creek. It was just as picturesque as the newspaper articles had said it was—and just as eerie. I drove until I came to an intersection and turned to see the low-slung building that housed the Sandy Hook Volunteer Fire and Rescue Company. I knew that this was the road that led to the elementary school where Adam Lanza, the twenty-year-old killer, massacred twenty-six people in eleven minutes with a semiautomatic rifle before turning the gun on himself. Like so many of these young male (often white) shooters, Lanza had a history of depression, which played out in social media broadcasts about his desire to kill innocent strangers.

I pulled into the empty parking lot of the fire department and sat there, my engine idling. Yellow barricade tape was strewn across the lot, which was riddled with puddles. I thought about how devastated everyone in this small, apparently close-knit town had been by these murders. Articles had said how locals who didn't lose a loved one were brought to their knees and left in a zombie-like stupor even years later. You have to see a village yourself, firsthand, even just passing through, to try to imagine how crushing a tragedy like this must be from the businesses boarded up in its tsunami wake. That's what all of this was: a short exercise in mourning and stricken imagination to consider a surreal form of violence that is becoming the norm in an increasingly unhinged America. My thoughts turned to my little boy. How could they not? Through tears and rage, I pledged to him that I would never take my eyes off of him, if I ever sensed his emotional distress. And I try to do the same thing for my male students. To the extent that I'm able, I keep an eye on them for their own well-being, as well as for the rest of us.

Since that evening in Newtown, my antennae have been up, searching for articles about mass shootings. I read them with a parent's irrational belief that knowledge and awareness are somehow amulets enough to shepherd our children safely into adulthood.

For the first time, many psychologists, sociologists, and criminal justice pundits are scrutinizing teen and twenty-something boys' lives with the cold-sweat urgency of epidemiologists struggling to contain a pandemic. These social scientists are searching for reasons why men continue to target their communities with unspeakable violence and carnage, from homicides and mass shootings to cases of sexual assault and rape. What they are finding is that this concerning uptick in violence is often the result of male perpetrators masking a perceived failure in their masculine identity.

An FBI report found that, since approximately 2007, the number of mass shootings in this country has more than doubled. Four of the five shootings with the largest numbers of victims occurred in the last five years. Data from the Gun Violence Archive reveals that a mass shooting occurs, on average, nine out of every ten days. Over the past four years, I've had two students from different high schools who have survived mass shootings.

When the Columbine tragedy occurred, Peter Langman was

working on his PhD in psychology. The notorious high school shooting immediately became his focus. "Or obsession," he told me. To try to make sense of mass shooting, he created an online database, SchoolShooters.info, which today includes 416 documents and more than 57,000 pages that chronicle cases from the past twenty years. After poring over the profiles of 133 murderers, Langman concluded that school shooters all suffer from a sense of what he calls "damaged masculinity." They have experienced romantic failures. They have endured falling short in the classroom. They suffer from the belief that they're failures as men because of their body shape, their size, or other body-image issues. At the same time, they lack empathy, are quick to rage, and feel an overwhelming sense of entitlement. These latter characteristics overlap with the same qualities we normally associate with hypermasculine jocks and hookup party boys. While shooters typically don't enjoy the same kind of social cachet as do boys in both of these categories, all shooters experience these "damaged masculinity" characteristics in varying degrees. However, a lack of empathy and entitlement are common threads among all of them. If slighted in any way, real or imagined, these shooters believe that someone else has to pay for their suffering.

In his research and writing, Eric Madfis, an associate professor of criminal justice at the University of Washington, Tacoma, has found that "depression and suicidal ideation are the most common mental health issues in backgrounds of men who kill." What about other severe forms of mental illness, such as psychosis or schizophrenia? Aren't they a bigger problem behind this epidemic of school violence? Madfis, the author of *The Risk of School Rampage: Assessing and Preventing Threats of School Violence*, dismisses them entirely. These forms of mental illness are "a lot less common than people think—a minority of [these killers] have severe forms of mental illness," he said. "School shooters often aren't very popular. They've been rejected by girls. They've been bullied. They blame everyone else for their failures in life. This is a profile that's different than serial killers or single incident homicidal killers." What often happens, according to Madfis, is that a "straining event precipitates these attacks. These guys don't just snap. There usually is a catastrophic event. A blow to one's masculinity."

In his article "Shame, Guilt, and Violence," psychiatrist and renowned violence researcher James Gilligan riffs on his vast experiences with violent men. "I have been struck by the frequency with which I received the same answer when I asked prisoners, or mental patients, why they assaulted or even killed someone. Time after time, they would reply 'because he disrespected me.'" In fact, these men employed this phrase so often they abbreviated it: "'He dissed me.'" Gilligan spent twenty-five years counseling and conducting research in the American prison system, exploring the root causes of violent behavior in men—from armed robbery to murder to sexual assault and rape. The author of the groundbreaking and seminal book on this topic, *Violence: Reflections on a National Epidemic*, discusses how he always thought that people committed armed robberies for the money. "But when I actually sat down and spoke at length with men who had repeatedly committed such crimes, I would start to hear comments like 'I never got so much respect before in my life as I did when I pointed a gun at some dude's face.'"

Being treated with respect is a big deal for all people—in jobs, in relationships, by store clerks and restaurant servers, and the list goes on. But many boys and men who live in environments where old-school masculine norms predominate, especially in neighborhoods where drugs, crime, and violence are a lifestyle, are forced into the kind of toxic masculinity that's championed in hypermasculine fields like the military and police work. Talk to any boy or young man who lives in such an environment and he'll tell you: if you don't put on your "armor" the second you leave your front door and walk and talk like the other guys running the streets, you're emasculated, considered a "punk," bullied, beaten up, dismissed, and disrespected. This may look a little different in rural communities, but the expectations are ultimately the same. Boys and young men growing up in the suburbs similarly experience the same kind of masculine shame; they may have more latitude in the superficial trappings of their identity, but beneath that they still feel the need to react with the same toxic violence when they feel that their masculinity is under siege. This is why so many of them are picking up semiautomatic rifles.

For many men, respect from their peers increases their sense of pride in their own masculine worth. Gilligan recounted a story about a hostile prisoner who, the more he was thrown into solitary confinement, the more violent he acted. Gilligan asked him what he wanted to get from acting out. "'What do you want so badly that you are willing to give up everything else in order to get it?' It seemed to me that this was exactly what he was doing. In response, this man, who was usually so inarticulate that it was difficult to get a clear answer to any question, astonished me by standing up tall, looking me in the eye, and replying with perfect clarity and a kind of simple eloquence: 'Pride. Dignity. Self-esteem.' And then, speaking more in his usual manner, he added, 'And I'll kill every motherfucker in that cell block if I have to in order to get it.'" The inmate went on to describe how he felt the officers were stripping away his last shred of dignity and self-esteem by disrespecting him. According to Gilligan, the man told him, "I still have my pride and I won't let them take that away from me. If you ain't got pride, you got nothing." Gilligan noted that the man "made it clear to me that he would die before he would humble himself to the officers by submitting to their demands."

To many people, this sounds like nothing more than a man trying to cling to his last-remaining ounce of dignity. And what's wrong with that? Nothing, of course. But when it becomes an obsession, a constant need to have everyone in your sphere, both intimates and strangers, terrified that they might accidentally disrespect you with some tiny unintended slight, well, that's a different story.

It's foolish and grossly inaccurate to assume that pathologically violent men are the only ones who are quick with their fists or the trigger over perceived slights. Lots of men who will never see the inside of a prison are guilty of this. For *all* men who share this trait, something else underlies their addiction to constantly seeking the respect they "deserve." This is what we always need to remember about swaggering, belligerent men who constantly insist upon respect: their sense of self-worth doesn't come from a place of deep, healthy, and generative strength. It comes from a far different source.

Shame. It *always* comes from shame.

As a culture, we don't second-guess or question violence coming from the hands of men, unless it's directed at women, children, or other innocent victims. Even then, it's usually too late for the victims. When violence occurs between two "consenting adults," as we like to think of the men engaged in it, we typically think of it as normal, their birthright even. Regardless of the "reasons" so many men break into violence—from the willingness to throw punches over a beer accidentally spilled on one's shirt to the willingness to endure months of harrowing solitary confinement over "disrespect" in prison to the willingness to kill innocent people because of rejection from young women or an employer—the root cause is shame.

Gilligan said that, after a quarter of a century of interviewing and counseling many of the most violent inmates, one of the most common "fantasies" he heard was a "scenario of going to their deaths in a hail of gunfire while killing as many people as possible."

This is why so many men either turn the gun on themselves after they've murdered, just as Adam Lanza did, or purposely get into shootouts with police with the goal of antagonizing them into unleashing a hail of bullets. "Indeed," wrote Gilligan, "this phenomenon is so common that police forces around the country (whose members often hate having to deal with these situations and are themselves traumatized by the outcome) have given it a nickname: 'suicide by cop.'" The goal in these situations isn't necessarily to kill police officers but rather to have a culturally sanctioned representative of the law (which the criminal is knowingly breaking) offer some lifeline to salvaged self-respect. It's the same perception younger boys have when they ape violent television shows or movies and pretend to die with toy guns, and it's the same when young men dream of "proving" themselves in battle—as if there's masculine glory and redemption in their sacrifice.

Gilligan said that men who fantasize about and actually go to such lengths are so "tormented by feelings of being shamed and disrespected by their enemies that they are willing to sacrifice their bodies and their physical existence to replace those intolerable feelings with the opposite feelings of pride and self-respect." They believe that dying is a way of not having to live with overwhelming feelings of shame. But if they allow themselves to be killed, well, at least other men they respect will consider this an honorable death, so they believe that pride and dignity will be their legacy.

According to Gilligan, shame is "the pathogen that causes violence."

This is why we are witnessing the explosive rage and violence among so many young men in Arabic countries.

In his book *The World Is Flat*, author and *New York Times* columnist for global affairs Thomas Friedman cites passages from a 2003 speech delivered by Malaysian prime minister Mahathir Mohamad to fellow Muslim leaders. He spoke to them about why their civilization had become so humiliated. "I will not enumerate the instances of our humiliation," said Mahathir. "Our only reaction is to become more and more angry. Angry people cannot think properly. There is a feeling of hopelessness among the Muslim countries and their people. They feel they can do nothing right."

Friedman, a three-time Pulitzer Prize–winning journalist, took this inextricable link between humiliation and rage in younger Arabic men a step further in *The World Is Flat*. "This humiliation is the key. It has always been my view that terrorism is not spawned by the poverty of money. It is spawned by the poverty of dignity. Humiliation is the most underestimated force in international relations and in human relations. It is when people or nations are humiliated that they really lash out and engage in extreme violence. . . . As my friend the Egyptian playwright Ali Salem said of the 9/11 hijackers, they 'are walking the streets of life, searching for tall buildings—for towers to bring down, because they are not able to be tall like them.'"

As long as there has been violence, this "pathogen" has existed. And vice versa. It's universal, and it drives the chronic incidences of male-on-male homicides and violence against women. Researchers who have studied FBI homicide reports from 1976 to 2017 found that deadly violence between intimate partners has risen disturbingly. Since 2010 this trend has increased by 26 percent; in 2017 women were far more likely to be murdered than men. The study also emphasized rising rates of females who commit violence against their partners. According to the National Coalition Against Domestic Violence, while one in three women have experienced some form of physical violence from their intimate partners—slapping, shoving, pushing—one in four men in heterosexual relationships have, as well. Two in five gay or bisexual men will also experience this.

The demographic that rarely gets mentioned in this discussion is children. They cannot dodge this bullet, either, even if they aren't

directly on the receiving end. Children exposed to domestic violence are more likely to attempt suicide later in life, abuse drugs
and alcohol, run away from home, engage in teenage prostitution,
and commit sexual assault crimes later on. And boys who witness
incidents of domestic violence as children are three to four times
more likely to commit violence against their partners when they
reach adulthood.

While the homicide numbers are unnerving, they pale in comparison to the recent rise in cases of sexual assault against girls and
women. One in five women will be the victim of sexual assault, rape,
or attempted rape in their lifetime. One in five. Department of Justice studies show that girls and young women between the ages of
twelve and twenty-four experience rape from males more often than
any other age group, while women of color are abused and sexually
assaulted at higher rates than white women.

Beneath much of the violence against women lies masculine
shame. Though there are many factors that can trigger this feeling,
the most common are perceived inadequacy in sex or at keeping a
job, fear of losing a female partner to another guy, and fear of looking bad in front of other men because of something a woman says
or does. Regardless, the violence is often invoked as an attempt at
masking feelings of inadequacy at playing the part of a man. It's a
desperate attempt at identity redemption.

Perhaps *the* X factor for women threatened with violence lies in
the proliferation of guns. Research shows that the presence of a gun
increases the likelihood of domestic homicide by *500 percent*, which
is why researchers believe these lethal statistics will only continue to
rise. According to the Pew Research Center, approximately 22 percent of women report owning a gun, while 62 percent of males report
owning one. Given that the brains of young men today are maturing
later, into their late twenties and even early thirties, which means

they are impulsive for longer than in the past, the combination of more guns and reactivity is a lethal causal relationship.

But there's something else driving this reactivity, something stemming more from the way boys and men are taught to handle rejection. In a *Psychology Today* blog about rejection, psychologist Suzanne Degges-White discusses how women internalize rejection and work hard to get over it. Ultimately, this can build emotional resiliency. Men, however, don't embrace the same inner scrutiny. They feel that their masculine identity has been attacked, and they externalize their feelings of shame from rejection, looking to "get even," Degges-White said. It's the same reaction to shame that Gilligan observed, and it erodes men's emotional resiliency.

We're starting to see what this looks like as we read about young, largely white males who swarm to internet "incel" sites where they lament their "involuntary celibacy," claiming they have been rejected for too long by attractive young women. Many of these young men obsess over their "unmasculine" physical features (chins, noses, foreheads, wrists, penises) in ways that Langman is all too familiar with. "Women and society have dejected us into loneliness and depression," one anonymous incel writer posted. "Their obsession with looks has driven many of us who don't fit their standards to anger and homicidal tendencies."

This is the volatile logic behind a small but disturbing number of young men who are seeking their revenge on the world, particularly targeting young women. Elliot Rodger was one of the most infamous examples of this. The twenty-two-year-old posted a manifesto online that echoed the feelings of many incel adherents—he railed about not having a girlfriend, about the impossible standards of attractive young women, and about having to witness happy couples (especially interracial ones), and he outlined his plans for "retribution." Rodger put this into action near the campus of the

University of California, Santa Barbara, when he murdered six men and women and wounded fourteen others by stabbing, shooting, and running them down with his car. He tried to enter a sorority house but couldn't gain access. Before police finally caught up with him, he shot and killed himself. In the video manifesto he said, "If I can't have you girls, I will destroy you."

John Douglas was a profiler with the FBI, where he studied the personalities and motives of the nation's most dangerous, notorious criminals. In his book *The Anatomy of Motive*, Douglas blamed the epidemic of violence on our easy access to guns and a growing degree of narcissistic reflexes in people today, which informs the "current climate of acting out one's rage in scenarios of indiscriminate violence." Narcissism helps explain why people who once might have committed suicide now point the gun at others. Instead of holding themselves accountable and exercising inner restraint, they blame other people for their problems, real or imagined. This squares with the massive spike in narcissism that researchers have observed throughout Western societies and, especially, in the US. Psychologists Jean Twenge and W. Keith Campbell surveyed more than 15,000 college students and compared their attitudes against the Narcissistic Personality Inventory. The Inventory measures narcissism among the "normal" population, not those who suffer from narcissistic personality disorder (NPD). They found that narcissism scores have more than doubled since the 1980s. A National Institutes of Health study of 35,000 Americans found that one in ten people in their twenties suffer from NPD. Other research has found that men of all ages are more likely to score higher in this extreme metric, especially men of color, but that women are starting to catch up. Douglas observes that the violent acts of such criminals are "the result of a deep-seated feeling of inadequacy." That is, deep-seated shame.

Gilligan says that violent people typically experienced abusive childhoods—ranging from physical abuse to bullying to taunting to ridicule to rejection to being starved or abandoned. "And I am far from being alone in noticing this," he wrote. "[M]any other psychiatrists who have studied murderers have reported the repeated and overwhelming shame and humiliation in their childhood experiences."

George knows all about this. The Northern California native's father left home when he was ten in the 1960s. While his mother was able to keep her large family intact, the huge void came at a great cost, as it often does. She worked a swing shift in the local cannery so she could send her children to school each morning. George told me that once she left the house, "I was thrown to the wolves." His older brothers wired him up to a battery and repeatedly shocked him. They threw him down small cliffs behind their farm. They shot at him with small-caliber guns. They even tied him to the bumper of their tractor and dragged him through the fields.

"They beat the shit out of me," he said.

Once, they made him stand on a stack of Folgers coffee cans under a laundry line in the family's backyard. After they tied a noose around his neck, they kicked the cans out from under him. "Nobody was supposed to help me. I was supposed to get down myself. Luckily, when my brothers left me, some of my sisters got me down. I was unconscious."

Later, after an older girl down the street sexually molested George, his brothers congratulated him on becoming "a man."

Every night George waited for his mother to come home from work. They had a "special" bond, he said, and George recalled how he "always wanted to be what she wanted from me—to be her good boy." But he never told her what happened. "I was too scared, too ashamed." Like many boys and men before and after him, George turned his shame and humiliation into violence. "I learned to give it back harder than I received it."

———

For many boys and men, shame is like a nerdy cousin they're forced to hang out with and can't ditch without severe consequences from a parent. It's an intolerable state that most males want to get rid of as quickly as possible because they fear other people will catch a whiff of their vulnerability. What better way to throw off this scent than to prove, at least incontrovertibly for that moment, one's perceived manly honor with a quick, explosive gesture? This is why, Terry Real told me, "the dynamic of male violence is always a [dramatic] shift from shame to grandiosity." We don't question its scale or severity because, after all, this notion of self-regeneration through violence "is a ceremonial performance of manhood," said Real. This is the "pathogen" Gilligan talks about, the perceived strength that impulsive boys and men lean on, especially when there's emotional pain from their past. Their perception of revenge is the shadow side of the trauma coin. "There are two ways trauma can go," Real said. "If you can sit in your own sense of vulnerability and be with your feelings, it will heal over time. But if you're unwilling to sit with and face it, you will turn towards grandiosity" and consider yourself a "self-righteous victim. And you will retaliate."

That said, Real doesn't consider many of these mass shooters to be suffering from extreme forms of mental illness, including paranoid schizophrenia. "Pathology is rarely an aberration of the norm," he said. "It's an exaggeration of the norm. These men and boys are not outliers. They are on the outer border. But they're made of the same stuff as you and me."

Real said that these young men are "buying into that [masculine] binary that you're either dominated or the dominator. Sure, it's an extreme reaction, but a lot of us do this same behavior to a lesser degree. When I lash out at my wife because she's telling me all the things I've been doing wrong, I feel victimized on some level. And on a bad day, I may yell back. It's the same impulse. But here's the difference. Many of us don't take it to the extreme that these other men and boys do."

(In the past, this "dominator" mindset was more common at a macro-level; white boys and men primarily saw "other" groups—think: Communists or people of color, Jewish males—as the threat. This still exists. But today this need to dominate occurs more pervasively at the interpersonal level. Boys and young men consume it and are schooled about it in the popular culture, especially violent video games and action-hero movies. Social media teaches girls and young women to be the "dominator.")

What few experts have looked at in this discussion is the decrease in emotional resiliency and, concomitantly, the rise in narcissism among younger teens and adults. Regardless of why boys and young men today are struggling, it's clear that the way they're externalizing stressors isn't working—and not just for them, but for the rest of us, too.

I recently heard a story on Vermont Public Radio about an eighteen-year-old boy who was arrested for plotting to "shoot up" his school. In preparation, he wrote out a kill list and purchased a 12-gauge pump shotgun. A big fan of the Parkland massacre, the boy, who struggled with ADHD and depression, kept a journal called "Diary of an Active Shooter." He had been making progress at a facility in Maine that helped him with his mental illness, but now that he was home in Vermont and navigating the problems and boredom of everyday life, he spiraled back into depression. "It's like why not end it a lil [sic] early," he posted on social media.

I don't think it's a stretch to say that this worldview, while extreme, mirrors the feelings of many young men who would rather sit home and game than work jobs that bore them, feel pointless, aren't cool enough, and don't bring in enough income to make them feel more powerful. Even the boys who look and act so differently from the alpha males who torment them are ultimately after the same kind of power.

———

Standing against a brick wall two weeks before he was supposed to be released from San Quentin State Prison, George felt something suspicious—and familiar. "You can feel the funk in the yard if you've been in prison before," George told me during a telephone interview. "The air was thick with tension. It wasn't anything you could easily see. It's just a heaviness and tension when you know something is about to go down. Everyone picks up on it, even the guards."

Someone among the Norteños, a Latino gang from Northern California, had ordered a hit on a white member of the Southerner gang. A profusion of violence and blood resulted. When the guards finally got things under control, prison administrators accused George, a member of the Norteños, of calling the hit. They had legitimate reason. George had done time in a revolving door of such "hard yards" as New Folsom, Soledad, Solano, Susanville, and Jamestown, where there was "a lot of banging" and he "ran yards," he told me. "I preferred that. I always wanted to make it home to my family and didn't want to be led by fools. So I spoke up to become a leader and ran yards and led riots. That was my comfort zone. That was what I knew."

This time, however, George hadn't made the call. "I was done with all that by this point," he said. Before his latest sentence, George had been drug-free, working and co-parenting for eight years, as well as accompanying his daughter to softball tournaments across the country. He was in prison this time for lapsing back into drug addiction, triggered by his mother's death and the ensuing estate battles with his brothers, which also kicked up old trauma.

During a committee hearing, George was allowed to make his case, but a prison lieutenant with whom George had "issues" did everything in his power to implicate him in the riot. The hearing erupted into a heated argument. "In the old days, I would have thrown the table aside and lunged at him. But I breathed slowly. Man, it was hard, but somehow I calmed myself and committed myself to beating him."

George lost his case and spent the next two years in around-the-clock isolation. Most men break under the duress and loneliness of solitary confinement. Not George. His commitment to "beating" the lieutenant meant not breaking down. As part of his commitment, he reevaluated his life trajectory for the first time. He sent away for books about nonviolent communication, determined to pick up on the education he had abandoned during high school and to prove the lieutenant—who always told George that he'd spend the rest of his life in prison—wrong.

Although George doesn't necessarily connect this inner shift with what happened after he was released from solitary confinement, it's hard not to perceive it as being tied to the tenet he would soon learn: love your fate.

Not long after he was released from solitary confinement, George was walking around the prison track one evening when he saw lights on in a building. He walked into the room. A "white dude" talking at the front greeted him. George took a seat in the back. *What's this guy's angle?* he wondered. "I spent a lot less time listening to what this dude was talking about than I did trying to figure out what he was after. He couldn't give a shit about any of us, I thought, because nobody cared."

This was at a time when Northern California correctional institu-
tions started opening their gates to a slew of nonprofit organizations
bent on helping inmates explore and work through the deeper psychological issues behind so much of their toxic behavior. "Suddenly,
San Quentin was filled with all these programs run by liberal white
people," said George. "I was a duck out of water."

Even though George didn't know them, he didn't trust these
white do-gooders. The mere idea of them triggered in him visceral
memories of a middle-aged prison administrator from his juvenile
home—a "dude in tasseled loafers and an alligator shirt"—who had
the "fucking nerve" to tell twelve-year-old George who he was and
what he needed to do with his life. Even though this man was probably trying to help him, George could only see the pain that white
people had caused him and his mother.

His father had been a pivotal organizer with Cesar Chavez's
United Farm Workers movement in California, which embraced
nonviolent civil disobedience. George recalled the iconic Chavez
meeting with his father in the basement of their family home, and he
vividly remembered taking part in the famous 300-mile march from
Delano to Sacramento, the state capitol, in 1966. "As we marched,
I saw a lot of white people throwing bottles and clods of dirt at my
mother," he recalled. He brought up this incident many times when
we spoke, a synaptic loop that haunts him; many decades later, it's
still the violence committed against her, not against his younger self,
that gnaws at him. As painful as this clearly was for George, it was
the surreal abuse his many older brothers inflicted on him—from
dragging him behind the tractor to the clothesline lynching—that
ultimately cast his die. "I grew up in a nonviolent movement, but I
became a very violent man."

By his own account, he was first arrested sometime between the
ages of ten and twelve. Today, his rap sheet includes numerous gang-

and drug-related crimes, as well as assault and battery charges. He told me he carried a machete in his pickup truck, used it, and was once jailed for beating a man senseless with a hammer.

Because of this history of violence—and his nearly lifelong mistrust of do-gooders—George returned to the class the next week and again after that, always with the same intention. "I was going to fuck him up," George told me. "I was going to get inside his head so everyone could see what a phony he was. I was rude and combative—I challenged things he said and even insulted him."

George then paused for a few moments. "But he didn't throw me out. No matter what I said or did, he remained calm the whole time. I couldn't break this guy. This really fucked me up, because, before, if something like this happened, I'd come at you with my fist or a knife."

As much as this guy unnerved George, he started to realize that he was different. "He was the real deal and really did want to help us." This terrified George, who wasn't ready to deal with issues that defined his life in and out of jail. As crazy as it sounds, George started to realize San Quentin wasn't the safe haven he had known for so long. That was when he decided that he had to do something to find his "center," the dysfunctional yet familiar inner base that had been his go-to since he was twelve. "I decided that I was going to get into trouble so I could get sent to [a different, more violent prison] where I'd be more comfortable."

But the "white dude" had other things in mind for George.

George doesn't remember when it happened, but within a month or so of attending classes, it became apparent that this white guy was "the first person to really care about us." That was when he let himself do something he hadn't done for a long time, let alone with a white person. He let himself trust.

The guy leading these classes was Dutch expatriate and former psychotherapist Jacques Verduin. The class was called GRIP (Guiding Rage into Power), a more finely tuned version of the Insight Prison Project (IPP) that Verduin had started in 1997. A groundbreaking curriculum that helped inmates with histories of violence, IPP helped men like George start to process and discuss their anger and rage. This required the men to learn something essential and foreign to them: accountability for the pain and suffering they caused, both for the victims, the victims' families, and their own loved ones. To help men dig into and examine their own trauma— long the source of their shame—Verduin later added a critical layer to the IPP program in 2012. This was the birth of GRIP.

It really was simple. Verduin wanted to help men break their relationship with violence through GRIP, and from what he discovered with IPP, this required developing emotional intelligence, cultivating mindfulness, and understanding what he calls "victim impacts," where inmates come face-to-face with victims or the families of victims who suffered the same crimes these men committed.

"There's a Navajo saying about 'offenders,'" Verduin said. "It means 'he or she who acts as if they have no relatives.'" These men, who disconnected from themselves at a young age, also disconnected from other people and, not surprisingly, lost the capacity for empathy. They lost their ability to feel accountable to a larger "tribe." For many men like George, this is what happens both literally and figuratively. "We try to help them restore the bonding of being part of a tribe," Verduin added, "which requires them to be more authentic and vulnerable. Really, that's the core goal: to help these men get in touch with their shame and to heal it."

Verduin and his facilitators begin GRIP classes at San Quentin and other prisons by telling inmates that they aren't there because of who they are or what they did. They tell the men that they're in prison because they believe the thoughts that justify their violent actions. "The goal behind this," Verduin told me, "is to deconstruct old belief systems, specifically the hypermasculine thoughts they've had their whole lives that led to [their imprisonment]." Within the first session or two of this year-long program, GRIP facilitators tell these men who have learned to see themselves as subhuman that they're not "monsters but people who radically forgot who they were," Verduin said. "We come together as a community to remind each other of who we are."

When George heard all of this, he said, "it just completely floored me, man. It made me realize I wasn't a throwaway. [Becoming so violent] wasn't entirely all my fault. That was when I wanted to learn." George's biggest breakthrough came when he took part in what's known as the "wheels" assignment. This is where GRIP students look at a visual that asks them to label and describe both their joys and pains on an illustrated wheel. This was the first time George had pried open the door on the sexual and violent physical abuse he suffered as a child. This was when he finally faced up to the realization that "by ten years old, I was already lost and abandoned. If it hadn't been for this assignment, I never would have gone back and thought about shit like that."

GRIP participants also learn mindfulness practices, which teach them the "SETA" acronym: becoming aware of and describing the physical sensations that arise when they feel anger; attaching that to an emotion or feeling; identifying the thoughts that run through their heads when anger arises; and, finally, sharing the action participants use to cope with the anger. This classic technique has been shown to put the skids on reactive anger and to increase empathy. A few years later, after his release from jail, George employed this technique to great effect. He was arrested and convicted on specious charges. After his appeal, he was found innocent. "Before GRIP, I would have told the judge, 'I don't recognize your robe or this court. Go fuck yourself.'

And I would have been thrown in prison for contempt. This time, I kept my cool, and years ago this case would never have even gone to an appeal because I would've been held in contempt of court and convicted by the judge, even though I was innocent."

Similar templates for trauma recovery work with male inmates exist in other prisons around the country, most commonly in California. Building Resilience is one such program. Founded and overseen by Stephanie Covington, codirector of both the Institute for Relational Development and the Center for Gender and Justice, this program operates in Corcoran and Pelican Bay, two maximum-security prisons, and the minimum-security California Institution for Men. It also has been exported to similar facilities for both men and women in the UK. Building Resilience, however, seems to be the only program tied to and guided by quantitative research. Nena Messina, a criminologist with UCLA's Integrated Substance Abuse Programs, conducted a study, which found that the program's focus on helping inmates work through their own trauma yielded positive outcomes of 90 percent, overall. Among the men who took part in the six sessions, which meet for an hour and a half to two hours twice a week, violence has decreased by 60 percent in Yard B at Corcoran, a Level 4 yard, which is the most dangerous. The men who took part in these sessions experienced lower levels of anxiety, depression, PTSD, aggression, anger, and one-on-one reactivity, among other positive outcomes. They also enjoyed greater mental health, social connectedness, and emotional regulation in five or six measures.

Once George started absorbing GRIP's lessons, life didn't suddenly shift and become easier. He and his new "tribe" had to navigate two radically different realities. For all of the healing and existential value he found in GRIP, life in prison outside that classroom was still lethal. It was still a world of violent men eager to prove their worth. Gangs devoted much of their time to militarizing their existence.

They worked out to build up their bodies; they wore their boots everywhere, even in the shower ("Always be suited and booted" went the mantra); they taught each other such military tactics as learning where the body's arteries were in case of hand-to-hand combat; they wore towels tightly wrapped around their necks coming out of the shower to protect their jugulars; they woke every hour to make sure they were safe in their cells. Clearly, what George and his classmates practiced and learned in GRIP created cognitive dissonance in such an environment.

Eventually, George was released from prison. The transition hasn't been easy, though. He still struggles to adjust to his freedom. For instance, he still wakes up often during the night, has chronic health problems from his long stint in solitary confinement, and occasionally finds himself twisting the towel around his neck after a shower. One of the few things that has grounded him is his work with GRIP; soon after George was released, Verduin sought out his help. These days, George is a lead facilitator and consultant for training. He loves going back to the prisons because, as he says, "I'm still one of them." This was why, on his first trip back to Avenal State Prison as a facilitator, he "froze as we went through the gate. I kept hearing a voice, saying, 'Get the fuck out of here. You're going to get killed. You're a gang member. You'll be fraternizing with the enemy you swore to kill.'" But he's learning to move beyond that old fear. When there was a riot at Avenal, the warden called in Verduin and George to help calm things down. And GRIP students there painted a mural of George. "Ain't nobody going to see it outside of prison but the people who matter most. They see it every day. That tells me I'm making a difference."

At fifty-nine, George still isn't afraid to fight. He's just become more judicious in which battles he chooses to fight, literally and figuratively. "I'll still get it on if I need to defend myself or my family."

But, in more urgent ways, he is a different man. "I always thought that being sensitive was being a pussy and a bitch," he told me. "Now I don't have a problem shedding a tear. If I'm sad, I fucking address it. I'll cry openly. And I'm willing to be compassionate with another man. You can be sensitive and still be a strong, capable man." He credits Verduin for all of this. "Jacques saved my life. I'd be serving a life term right now if it weren't for him. No question about it." In one of his rare moments without barbed words, George shared that "Jacques's a collector of people, and he told me that he wanted to collect me. I thank God he collected me and let me know that I have value. I have worth. It's a huge deal to get this from another man. Especially a white man."

By his own admission, George never would have said such a thing before he had gone through GRIP teaching and training. Until that point, the toxic version of masculinity that he employed as both "bulletproof" insulation and as a weapon didn't allow for this kind of vulnerability, which makes possible reconnecting with the deeper, truer self and, in turn, with others in authentic ways. But GRIP "cracked me open," he said. It revealed the healing and generative power in the soft underbelly of past trauma—the very thing toxic masculinity had taught him to fear, to attack in both himself and in others. This made it possible to reimagine, with honest, critical distance, what power could look like in a more healthy, sustainable, and beneficial form for himself, his family, his friends, and his community. It taught him that power could be constructive—that it should create and build, not destroy.

GRIP also taught him something equally crucial about power: the need for accountability. George has worked hard to understand something essential for men finding their own existential liberation. Far too many men must bottom out before they're willing to look within and to realize—and own—their role in their own downfall. Programs such as GRIP (and Jericho Circle) teach men how to be accountable for the harm they caused others and their communities—and themselves. That, these men learn, is a necessary step to creating the deeper, tougher courage and resiliency needed to stop the cycle of wanton violence.

George now takes great pride in being the kind of present father and grandfather that he wanted to be but wasn't always able to be, having spent so much time in prison. He's also proud that he's nearly completed his college degree. It's easy to envision a bit of his father in him, the absent activist, when he talks about his work with GRIP and, specifically, about the men he works with. The cadence of his speech picks up, as if he can't get all of the thoughts and feelings out of his mouth quickly enough.

"All I want to do is make change through these guys who were like me and need someone to listen to them and to show them the way." He gushed when he described what it's like to see a room full of embattled, violent men of all races—many of whom have taken oaths to fight and kill each other—open up and support each other and even cry. "That's fucking courageous. That's balls. Nothing but power coming out of these guys! My guys."

Not surprisingly, George's passion, zeal, and feverish commitment to helping men behind bars is ultimately about something else. Sure, he sees himself in them. He also clearly feels a debt of gratitude to Verduin for transforming and saving his life. Despite the unfathomable pain and suffering that his father's abandonment wrought for George and his entire family, from a distance he grew to respect his father's dedication to helping the downtrodden. Over and over again, though, George spoke about the "special, close relationship" he had with his mother, how much better he felt—despite the endless abuse from his own brothers that left him with PTSD—when she walked through that door every night. "She was my protector."

Now that George has exorcised decades of shame and has, in his own words, become a "productive member of society," he has come full circle. "My mom's looking down from heaven," he said. "You know what she's saying? Now my son is finally getting back to be the genuine, authentic man that he was supposed to be."

Our Brothers' Keepers

Something George told me during our interview has stayed with me.

"I thank God [Jacques Verduin] collected me," he said, referring to his mentor, the founder of GRIP.

An intelligent and grateful man, George is fiercely independent and still somewhat guarded, which makes sense. His life before GRIP was primarily defined by violence and a healthy distrust of author-ity figures, particularly white authority figures. Initially, George's unabashed trust in Verduin as his guardian, his keeper, surprised me. But, given how much faith, love, and admiration Verduin has for George, I got it.

"I thank God he collected me and let me know that I have value. I have worth," he said. "It's a huge deal to get this from another man. Especially a white man."

I didn't understand why George's comments stayed with me until I started writing this epilogue.

To solve the ongoing crisis of masculinity, I now realize, we need to learn how to be *all* of our brothers' keepers as men. We need to "collect" one another; that is, we need to learn how to extend ourselves to and support one another in ways that, historically, men haven't felt comfortable or safe doing or haven't felt permission to do. We need to replace unnecessary competition in our interactions with a proprietary sense of responsibility to help boys and also men feel more connected, less alone.

The boys and men profiled in this book offer models of what this can—and should—look like. Together and separately, their stories hold answers to the questions most troubling to us about what it means to be a man today. We should keep their stories close at hand, so we can share them as models of what a masculinity that has the courage and strength to act from a place of deeper humanity looks like.

No other circle of boys' lives is as central and defining as school. It's where most children spend a large part of their days, and it's where most of their early social development occurs. More than any other boys I interviewed, Nico and Harrison stood out. Now, they weren't that different from many boys in their group—or from a lot of boys out there who have been raised on greater self-awareness and empathy for women and people of color. What stood out about these two boys was that they had the courage to openly sift through their fears, their challenges, and their struggles as ascending young men. While most of the boys I interviewed didn't talk as candidly, Nico and Harrison both expressed their own doubts and vulnerabilities with the full knowledge that their search for a truer and more stable expression of their masculine identity wouldn't be welcomed outside of the group's classroom door.

Both boys show tremendous courage—courage that many men two, three, or four times their age couldn't muster beyond the closed doors of their men's groups. When I asked participants in men's groups whether they applied the deeper emotional honesty and vulnerability they discovered about themselves outside of the group, most of them said that they didn't. As sixty-something Jay told me, "It's not safe in the real world. If I share my feelings, they might be open to misinterpretation when there aren't the same ground rules."

This is the equivalent of training to become, say, an Olympic-ready snowboarder and never applying your talent outside of the secret practice run.

But Nico and Harrison did.

They found ways to bring their skills to bear *outside of the safe space*. Nico was questioning his place as a boy at the edge of adolescence in a world where females are ascending, while males are descending. He did this in the group and, to a greater extent, with me in our conversations together. And Harrison was finding ways to integrate his strong emotional reactions—including joy and sadness—into his life beyond the group. Considering that feelings beyond anger or frustration in males are often met with judgment, this was no small thing. Sometimes, even during group meetings, the other boys would smirk when Harrison openly demonstrated such feelings. To observe his face is to know that he is someone who feels things strongly, deeply, quickly. The last time I saw Harrison, he confessed that he was starting to realize that maybe his intense reactions were, in his words, sometimes "getting in the way." "I'm a lot like my dad," he said, referring to his big feelings and reactivity. "A lot of that I like." And it was also something he wanted to change. "Not just to fit in," he said. "I don't want my feelings to control me. But there's also a lot I like about feeling things strongly. I like to be honest about who I am. Authentic."

Being true to ourselves and authentic—and not to some mono-lithic idea of masculinity that more often than not prevents us from realizing our full potential as men—that's the point and the promise of this book.

Nico and Harrison are pushing themselves to redesign their burgeoning masculine identities in the real world, so that they align with how they perceive themselves, regardless of other males' expectations.

What they didn't realize when I interviewed them, though, was that this journey wasn't reserved for them. Nor was it reserved for the other boys and men I profiled in the previous pages. Their journeys help answer the existential questions about what it means to be male in the twenty-first century. Everyone benefits from their conscious and continued efforts to be better and more present boys and men by converting sensitivity, empathy, and vulnerability into sources of courage, strength, and emotional resiliency.

Of all the older boys I interviewed, Taylor stands apart for his abil-ity to cultivate this hidden strength. Like so many high school and older boys today, Taylor suffers from depression. Yet he has learned to deal with the X factor behind so much of the suffering older boys and men are experiencing, as well as the feelings of worthlessness that result from it.

Depression is one of the biggest contributing factors, perhaps the most overlooked, behind the epidemic of suicide for older boys and men. A crucial factor in this blind spot occurs because of our cul-tural insistence on viewing depression as a moral failure, a lack of inner strength and resiliency—a blatant submission to vulnerability. This is why many health-care practitioners don't or won't diagnose their male patients with depression; they don't want men to feel, as psychologist Terry Real said, that they're exposing men, that they're "pulling down [their] pants."

Complicating this, the diagnostic tools many health-care practitioners have relied on for measuring depression have largely focused on symptoms that are more common to females—sadness, loss of appetite, ennui, crying jags. While men do experience some of these symptoms, depression in many men manifests through such different reactions as angry outbursts, irritability, and increased risk-taking behaviors. This is why depression in males is often mis- and underdiagnosed. If this weren't bad enough, males as young as elementary school know that they're not supposed to ask for help. Regardless of whether boys or young men adhere closely to such conventional, limiting expressions of masculinity, they consider themselves "failures" if they admit that they need help.

With the help of a friend from his calculus class—and Tony Robbins's books—Taylor found respite from his depression. He now keeps a gratitude journal, which he updates every night, ending the day on a positive note. "The clouds of depression are always there," he said, "but when I do all of these things they start to dissipate. And I can see who I'm supposed to be."

As someone who has taught Taylor in the college classroom, I can vouch for this transformation. Between his freshman and junior years, he became a different young man. By junior year he was far more outgoing and talkative during class discussions, he handed in assignments on time, and his writing smacked of a confidence and incisiveness he lacked only two years earlier. He had really started coming into his own.

When we talk with the adolescents and young men in our circles going through the same struggles as Taylor, we should share his story to let them know that they aren't alone or deficient or without options. Taylor's story can be a source of inspiration for what's possible.

We should share, too, the story of Anthony Carpenter, the

counselor at Becoming a Man in Chicago. The Calm Lion is helping young men around the same age as Taylor develop the skills to regulate their emotions, improve their recognition of other people's emotional states, and figure out how to work through their tensions with other people, calmly and constructively.

———

Nearly all of the men who agreed to be interviewed for this book had a vested interest in doing so. They had moving personal stories about their own suffering that they hoped might somehow help other boys or men. Chris was the exception. The emergency room nurse didn't share any gripping stories or hard-won wisdom. But he brought to our interviews a commitment and willingness that always matched that of the men who gave unselfishly of themselves, over and over.

Perhaps not surprisingly, Chris was a bit of an enigma. Here was this thirty-five-year-old Iraq War ex-infantryman who still proudly considered himself "army-tough," working in a career that his army buddies still made fun of after six years and that legions of working-class men from similar backgrounds would never consider as an option for themselves. They are the masses of unemployed men we've read about who suffer from high rates of alcoholism, opiate addiction, and suicide. They would rather cling to the old ways of expressing their masculinity, even if it prevents them from securing gainful and fulfilling employment in growing industries that have historically been female-dominated.

But Chris is proving that men can enter into such career fields without sacrificing their masculine identity. In fact, Chris found great satisfaction and a greater sense of his self by leaning into the same personal characteristics and professional skill sets we too often dismiss as "feminine." He showed that there's nothing unmanly or limiting about practicing collaboration, good communications skills, compassion, and empathy. His efforts prove that it's entirely possible to break free from static expressions of masculinity to discover new passions and realize greater professional satisfaction. "[Nurses are] the ones families see when a baby is born, and we're the ones they see when a parent dies," he observed. "I like being there for my patients and their families at such times."

Chris is an inspiration, a model of modern masculinity that allows him to live his most authentic life and express his best self through his work. Share his story with the men in your life who are either reluctant to take on untraditional or service-oriented (read: "uncool") jobs or who continue to hold out for traditional "manly" jobs that are slowly disappearing today.

———

Many people would look at Paul's private life and shake their heads, perhaps even feel a twinge of embarrassment. After all, here is a grown man in his early sixties who was so desperate for affection that he hugged a vertical beam in his apartment. Many times. And today he goes out to dinner by himself, sometimes "literally to have someone to talk to when I order food. Or just to be around other people."

At a time when more and more people are carrying food out of restaurants because they are simply terrified of being seen eating alone, Paul is doing something that people don't even realize shows courage, not to mention emotional resiliency. But it does. Perhaps most important, he is bucking a loneliness epidemic that is overwhelming men and that has disastrous repercussions for them. More than 200 studies worldwide have found that chronic loneliness can cause life-threatening illnesses. It also leads to social and emotional isolation, which can lead to depression and, if untreated, suicide.

This chain reaction is far more of a threat in men who, other studies show, maintain only one or two close friendships and rarely confide in these male friends the way they do with wives or female partners. Given the increasing numbers of single men, that means more and more of them have no one in whom they can confide about their deeper issues and feelings that they otherwise swallow back.

Even men who have wives, partners, or girlfriends don't maintain their close male friendships as well as women do. The Male Deficit Model speaks to this; research shows that when men aren't physically seeing their friends, they lose touch and, in turn, sacrifice the deeper emotional connection they once enjoyed.

The bottom line is this: there is no magic to creating and maintaining the deeper, more intimate friendships men need to keep loneliness and social isolation at bay. Friendships also don't operate on auto-pilot the way they do when we're younger. They require time and effort. Paul learned that he had to push beyond the old, comfortable, static masculine norms he once followed. "I've got to be honest with myself if I'm going to move forward," he told me. "I can't ignore or push my feelings down anymore."

As Paul illustrates in bald, sometimes awkward but always courageous acts, making and maintaining friendships isn't pretty. It requires risk. Sometimes it feels lonely or desperate. But his dogged pursuit of companionship and friendship is a blueprint more men could greatly benefit from following. Share his story with the men in your life who are struggling to maintain relationships, the men who are slowly drifting away in isolation.

———

When I heard George's life story, I immediately thought of Joseph Campbell. The mid-twentieth-century academic, whose corpus of work explored comparative religion and mythology, penned the seminal book on hero archetypes, *The Hero with a Thousand Faces*. In it, Campbell unpacks the classic trajectory for the hero's journey: the call to adventure, supernatural aid, the many struggles, the desire to turn back and to renounce the journey, the transformation, the atonement, and the return to the hero's community with greater wisdom and healing. George's life squares neatly with this trajectory.

What so many boys who grow into violent men aren't ready to realize is that the foundation of all of their rage and violence is shame. This was the groundbreaking discovery psychiatrist James Gilligan made over twenty years of working in American prisons and in his book, *Violence: Reflections on a National Epidemic*. Gilligan learned that when males lash out with hostile words and actions, it's almost always because they feel disrespected or some other form of rejection. It's a thin-skinned reactivity rooted in the toxic masculine need to *always* appear strong, respected, and in control. Very close to this thin-skinned surface lies a deep reservoir of shame, often from having said or done things at a younger age and being made to feel profound guilt for not "measuring up" as a man. Reacting with violence, they learn, is a sanctioned way to seemingly reclaim their masculine status in the eyes of males they respect.

This is an integral factor in what's fueling the present epidemics of mass shootings, violence against women, and homicides in too many poor neighborhoods, especially those filled with young men of color.

George spent five decades of his life in and out of prison, as part of a gang from Northern California. He was, he told me, a "very violent man." All of this came to a halt after he encountered Jacques Verduin and his new GRIP program. This was when George began to follow the thread to his own victimization as a young boy and understand how it, and the hypermasculine expectations of how he should respond to it, influenced his toxic path. And he learned about the Navajo saying that describes "offenders" as people who act as if they have no relatives. As if they have no larger family. As if they have no accountability. George learned and took these lessons to heart—and walked away from the violence that had defined much of his life. Today, he shepherds other men on this hero's journey in GRIP through their own trauma and the deep-seated shame that fueled the violence they inflicted on so many others, as well as on themselves.

This is why we need to "collect" and hold close the boys and men in this book. They are guideposts, so to speak, on the path to the most heroic and necessary journey boys and men will ever undertake: the quest for the kind of courage, strength, and resilience they need and we need from them.

Letter to My Son

My dearest son,

It's late, you're asleep, and so is Mama. I'm still up, because I'm trying to think of the words I want to share with you but didn't this afternoon when you grew inconsolably angry. It was yet another example of a reaction you had to a small incident that leaves me worried. Why am I worried about something that, admittedly, was a blip that neither one of us will remember? Because the longer Mama and I wait to help you work through the "big" feelings that sometimes overwhelm you, the harder it will be for you to handle them a few years down the road—at a point in life when bigger boys act on such feelings in ways that sometimes harm themselves and often hurt others.

By the time you're old enough to read and understand this letter, you will have long forgotten what I'm talking about here. So, I'll recap what happened. On the car ride home today, you were very upset and had that wounded look you get on your sweet little face, the one where you stare out of the car window, looking as if a rug was yanked out from beneath you. In a sense, it was. Eventually, you shared with me that one of your first-grade friends, Luke, had cut in front of you to take a turn at bat during kickball.

"I thought he was my friend!" you barked. "Friends don't do things like that to each other."

"I think it's great you're thinking about what makes for a good friend," I responded. "But Luke probably didn't even realize that he had done it. I bet it was an accident."

Arms crossed, lips pursed, vigorously shaking your head as you continued to look out the window, you weren't having any of it. Then I suggested something that I'm only learning to do now in middle age. "Maybe tomorrow you can tell Luke that what he did hurt your feelings, because it sure seems like it did," I said in the car.

When you heard this, you practically exploded from your car seat. "I knew you were going to say that!" you bellowed. "Words don't work, Dad! They don't take them seriously." Then you grew more up-set. "Telling them I'm going to beat them up with karate is what gets them to stop," you yelled, your voice breaking as tears welled up in your eyes like little knots. (Already you are following in the footsteps of too many men who lump people into a generic and convenient "they" out of hurt.)

"Did he hurt your feelings?" I asked. Long silence. No head movement. "Did he?" I asked again. You nodded, still looking out the window at the winter trees in all of their bare, angular truth.

I know that the way you felt and handled your hurt on this after-noon may not seem like a big deal. It wouldn't to many, maybe most, people. After all, you are only seven. But tacitly accepting this "boys will be boys" worldview starts a runaway train in explosive thoughts and behaviors that few boys, eventually men, ever reverse for the rest of their lives. You'll witness this when you get older, if you haven't already, how the only time men look within and question their behavior or worldview is when they face tragedy: a wife, partner, or girlfriend walks out on them; they become addicted to something and lose their career, home, and maybe their family; they develop a serious illness. There's a sudden awakening. Otherwise, there is no reason to change a way of being in the world that nearly everyone directly or indirectly condones and that *seemingly* has served them up to that point. When you see males going through this, ask yourself: Why don't most women who face personal strife also experience this sudden emotional implosion?

Since you were five, you have been making comments and asking questions about war, fighting, and death. The questioning has grown more frequent this year. I've been wracking my brain trying to understand why. After all, Mama and I don't allow you to play violent video games, nor do we allow you to watch violent cartoons or television shows. And we always encourage you to "Use your words"—and to describe your feelings—instead of reaching for your fists or "fisted" words. (I don't know if, when you're old enough to read this, you'll remember how annoyed I used to get that all of your Lego figurines had grimaces and sneers.) This was why I lost my cool when you asked the seemingly innocent question one morning at breakfast, "Do they still shoot soldiers for running away during battles like they did during the Civil War?" "Could you please stop talking and thinking about violence all of the time?!" I snapped. This is something I find myself asking you, with varying degrees of patience, over and over.

What I didn't tell you is this: asking you to not think about violent things is like asking a cornered animal not to lash out. How do you put the skids on a survival skill? Now, I know from my own experience that extreme anxiety can lead to violent and morbid thoughts. But there's something else that triggers a lot of boys' violent thoughts and feelings that no one talks about: fear and the need to conquer it.

Contrary to the adult belief that being a child is easy and carefree, it's not. When you're young, especially if you're sensitive, insightful, and observant, as you are, the world can be a very scary place—and you're fairly powerless. Lashing out at the things that scare you gives the illusion of conquering and controlling them.

But there's another reason—one no one seems to talk about—that I'm convinced also stokes the volatile reactions of boys and, later on, men. Contrary to what we're all told about girls being more emotional than boys, most boys are born with far stronger feelings and emotions than girls are. What makes it even harder for boys is that many parents don't help them deal with these strong emotions. They teach them the opposite: to swallow them down, to hide them, because (1) parents think this helps prepare their sons for "manhood," and (2) too many adults think that older boys and men who show emotional vulnerability are ultimately failures as males. Like many boys, you don't know what to do with the "big feelings" you often feel. And you resist help working through them. This didn't make sense to me until recently. We were cleaning up your room, when you blew up at me for moving some of your Lego creations. I tried getting you to do some slow breathing, but you resisted—you resisted every attempt I made at helping you slow down and step back from your anger. When I asked why you didn't want to at least try any techniques for calming down, you shared something insightful, something I and many adults don't realize about boys. "I don't think I can," you said. "They're too powerful."

Since that enlightening moment, I realize that I also know about this, from firsthand experience. When I was your age, I got into a fistfight with another boy in my neighborhood named Georgie. He was one of the meanest boys I ever met, and that says a lot. He had lightning-white hair and narrow, slit eyes that slithered back and forth as he determined when and where he would strike. Fights in my neighborhood occurred, but they were functional—punches flew only until both boys exhausted their resentment, which was usually within a few minutes. No one ever walked away injured in body or in spirit. On this September day, though, things changed. Like me, Georgie was only seven or eight, but he unleashed a relentless barbarity on me that the crowd of assembled neighborhood boys and I had only seen, let alone imagined, in war movies. No matter where I ran to escape this brutal beating, Georgie hunted me down and continued until I was a battered mess.

When I made it through the back door of my home that afternoon, I finally felt some degree of relief. I was going to be met with compassion and concern, I thought. In my mother I would find succor, and in my oldest brother I would find protection.

What I heard, however, was my brother screaming that I was a "coward," that I was an "embarrassment," and that I was the "family black sheep." My mother met these accusations with silence and then said, "Well, maybe he'll outgrow this." I wouldn't. Couldn't. Until I was in my thirties, my oldest brother kept up a smear campaign that met with some degree of success with my father, much more with my mother.

I spent the rest of my childhood punching my way to redemption and, when I discovered the futility of that, spent the rest of my life brawling without fists for the very thing my family and so many other people pushed back against—carving out a manhood shaped by greater emotional honesty. And I have fought against the *real* coward: any male who attacks and shames sensitive males because he believes this will make him appear stronger, more manly.

This is one of many things I learned along the way: boys are taught to work hard, really hard, to mask their strong emotions and feelings because they know that they'll be judged harshly and rejected if they show them openly. Do you remember kindergarten or even the first few years of elementary school at all? Do you remember how the boys were the quickest ones to tears? How they openly showed the most frustration? How they hurled wounding words and punches if someone hurt their feelings or made them look bad in front of other boys? What you may not have known is that whenever boys feel emotionally disconnected from the rest of the class or their friends, they react in ways that make them feel redeemed, reinstated as a Man Card carrier. This, by the way, is something all boys and men learn to do—mask the scent of their vulnerability with actions or words that give the appearance of traditional masculine "strength."

You learned this during kindergarten yourself. How do I know? Because when I would pick you up from school, you always knew that I'd want to know how you got along with your friends and classmates that day. I don't know if you remember, but you struggled making and keeping friends. Like me, you feel things deeply; you show your love and compassion freely, as well as your hurt and your need for justice. It's an inner tug-of-war I sometimes wish I hadn't handed down to you. It's why you struggled with the way other children could be mean and unwelcoming when you encountered them for the first time at summer camps or on the playground. Kindergarten was the first year when you started acting like the other boys, when you sometimes pretended that other children's hurtful slights didn't faze you. You and I spent a lot of time on those car rides home, talking about how it was okay to feel hurt, how to let other children know that they said or did something that hurt your feelings, and how to set boundaries with them.

If there's anything you learn from me about all that I have ever shared with you, have tried to teach you, about what it means to be a *healthy* man, I hope it is this: so many older kids and adults, both men and women, will say and do many things to you and to other boys in the name of preparing you to become a man. They will tell you not to cry. They will give you disapproving glances if you show joy or sadness or shame. They will tell you, "Men don't (fill in the verb here) like that" when you feel the need for someone to know how you feel deep down (other than anger, of course). They will tell you to "suck it up," to "man up," or to "take it like a man" when your feelings are hurt, when you're in physical or emotional pain, when you feel like you can't handle a situation. In other words—and this is crucial to remember—they will try to make you feel *shame* for expressing the very feelings that make you a healthy man and human being. These are the people who believe that becoming a man means shutting off the pipeline to your deeper humanity because it "toughens you" and will make you a more competent man.

And they're patently wrong. Always.

Here's the secret too few adults know or, even if they do, will tell you. Closing off the pipeline to our deeper emotions and to feelings other than anger doesn't make boys into stronger, more competent men. It weakens them. It enervates and depletes boys and, eventually, men of the courage to "show up" and offer the people who need it most their sensitivity, their compassion, their empathy, and, yes, their vulnerability. The people who rely on us don't need yet more strength in our biceps: they need it in our hearts.

When you were first born, it was primarily Mama who took care of you. The main time you and I spent together, alone, was late at night, after she'd nursed you and could no longer console you. In the first two months or so, you'd wake up every night between eleven thirty and midnight. As a first-time father, I was terrified by this. I had no experience with babies. More urgently, I felt as if I couldn't calm you down, and this was a big problem. You would cry so hard that your poor little vocal cords would strain and grow hoarse. Finally, after an hour or more of this, you would pass out in exhaustion.

Mama showed me how to wrap you in one of those soft slings that kept you snug against my chest. She hoped that this might calm you a bit more. It didn't at first. One night, two months after you were born, I took you outside for a walk, hoping that the late night darkness and stillness would quiet you. I stopped behind a nearby elementary school, and we stood beneath the moon on the pitcher's mound of a baseball diamond. I lifted you out of the sling, facing me, to show you the moon, and you pounded against my chest with your tiny arms and legs until it felt like my sternum was cracking. In some small way, it did.

After that night on the baseball diamond, something shifted within me. I realized what it was a week or so later, while reading you children's books. For the first time I saw how so many fathers in these books were caricatures of what a "man" should be—they led their sons on adventures; they exhibited physical strength; they cracked goofy jokes or, in the more recent books, modeled "cool" behavior; and they often seemed clueless about many domestic duties. Most glaringly, they abdicated all nurturing and sensitivity to the female or mother characters. These were the traits that fathers—painted as heroes—embodied.

This was when I realized that as painful as it was to witness you in such a distressed state, I wasn't going to take the easy way out. I wouldn't be that father who was a storybook character. I would have to acknowledge the part of my chest where you "cracked me open" and find ways to show up for you—to grow into fatherhood and find ways to comfort and nurture you when and how you needed it. This was when I promised you that you would learn, firsthand, that fathers could equal mothers when it came to sensitivity and to nurturing, that this wasn't a matter of evolutionary wiring. This was when I committed to teaching you and myself that vulnerability really did make men stronger, tougher.

On those many nights after I had this epiphany, we'd walk through our neighborhood at one in the morning, you'd cry, and I'd pull you closer to my chest and do whatever it took to calm you and let you know that I was there for you. That was when I promised you that I'd always try to nurture you in ways that you needed, even if they weren't always comfortable or easy for me.

Please don't think for one second that, for all of my idealism and righteousness, I'm an ideal father. There are so many things I do wrong and model for you. I'm too reactive, too anxious, too indignant, too nonresilient many days. None of this would be a problem if I didn't see you watching and emulating me so closely. But I hope that I also model a way of being a man that is far more empowering, liberating, and healthy for you. I may not spend my time with you trying to make you laugh, going on adventures, or teaching you the value of being "cool."

But I will always encourage and support you on the quest to find a masculine identity that

gives you permission to love and take healthy risks without fear;

gives you greater emotional resiliency;

finds strength in vulnerability;

gives you deeper strength and courage;

teaches you to be accountable to yourself and to others;

and allows you to experience the full range of your deeper emotional life—the full spectrum of your humanity—without apology.

This, my son, is the *real* hero's journey.

As long as I have breath in my lungs, I will give you the love and nurturing that you need and desire, on demand. If there is anything you remember me for, I hope it is this: that I *always* fought the good fight for you . . . and for all boys and men.

ACKNOWLEDGMENTS

This book was born out of an email exchange, a conversation, really, with my editor Miles Doyle. In the spring of 2016, he reached out to me after reading a piece I wrote for the *New York Times* about the need for emotional honesty in men. He, too, saw the pressing need for males of all ages to develop a different kind of strength, courage, and resiliency that they need to thrive and survive—and that we need from them. More than four years later, I am deeply grateful for his curiosity, passion, and level-headed guidance and collaboration throughout the development of this book. I also want to thank Gideon Weil, who helped shepherd this book through its final lap with a savvy, crucial touch. And thank you to the production, marketing, and publicity teams at HarperOne for their brand of friendly, thoughtful expertise and professionalism, especially Melinda Mullin and Suzanne Quist, as well as Sam Tatum in editorial.

Ryan Harbage, my agent, has also been a great champion for healthy masculinity and a much-valued collaborator. He has been a well of sagacity and perspective over the past three years, both of which were deeply appreciated.

This book never would have seen the light of day—no way—without my wife, Elizabeth, my stepdaughter, Aliya, and my son, Macallah. Aliya's sharp observations about the shifts in girls' aggression were most helpful. The endless sacrifices and loving succor from Elizabeth and Macallah, when all were sorely needed, buoyed me. So did Elizabeth's willingness to pick up my slack on the domestic front—*no* small thing over three years with younger children.

Thank you to the many boys and men who agreed to be interviewed for this book. I am grateful for—honored by—the courage they showed in sharing their private, often painful, stories. And thank you to the many experts quoted in here. They, and these boys and men, understand the pressing need—now more than ever before—to embrace a new masculinity.

My friend Harry Legum modeled the kind of friendship many men need more of—an empathetic, patient ear; a willingness to talk about the joys, the struggles, and the sorrows; and judgement-free support. I'm also grateful for his "scholarship" dinners at the Prime Rib in Baltimore (and the Manhattans), which were as fortifying and rejuvenating as any spa.

My deep gratitude goes out to Wendy Smith, my sister, for her enlightened worldview and sisterly guidance throughout my life; it goes out to my brother Robert Reiner, sister-in-law Melissa Schneider, and niece Ellie Reiner for their humor and perspective; and it goes out to my dear old friends Dan Shear and Scott Timberg, the first people who insisted how necessary a book on this topic was.

My regrets: my mother, Barbara Reiner—my first, most steadfast supporter—would have radiated with joy and pride at this book if dementia hadn't erased her memory; and my father, Mitchell Reiner, who taught me how to love tenderly and fight fiercely, would have told me the words I never got to hear when he was alive: "You finally did it."

Roger and Bernice Kaufman, my in-laws, have been unrivaled in their support of my writing life for years and throughout this book process. Thank you both.

Thank you to David and Harriet Kaufman, my uncle and aunt, for their many forms of loving encouragement and support; to Eleanor Kaufman, my sister-in-law, for her photographic wizardry; to my supportive brother-in-law, Faraz Khan; to cousin Emily Kaufman and husband Mike Lewman for their many forms of loving-kindness; and to cousin Josh Kaufman and Anna Laubach, for hosting and feting me in Chicago.

The work of Bradley Fenner and John Kinniburgh at Prince Alfred College in Adelaide, South Australia, is inspiring. A big thank-you to them for their passion and commitment to collaborating on finding new ways to teach boys (and their parents) a healthier male identity. My gratitude also goes to these schools for all of their help in my research and with similar collaborations: the Sheridan School in Washington, DC; Stuart Ryan and the Shore School in Sydney, Australia; Avon Old Farms School in Connecticut; and St. Paul's School for Boys, the McDonogh School, and Boys' Latin School, all in Baltimore.

Phyllis Fagell and Teddy Wayne have been much-valued friends and fellow writers whose help and guidance have been much appreciated. Thank you to Jacques Verduin and George Luna for their considerable contributions. And thank you to Audrey Le and Sally Satterthwaite for their exceptional generosity and kindness in providing a stranger with a quiet place to write in sight of Mount Desert Island.

INDEX